Told
The Art of Story

Told
The Art of Story

Stories and photographs by Simon Aboud
Story principles by Paul Wilson

Booth-Clibborn Editions

CONTENTS

Told is a celebration of story, its timeless principles and how they make you feel. This is a book about the emotion of storytelling. Storytelling is anything but logical.

It is designed to show you story's power: how it teaches us lessons and makes its points, how it moves the rational to the emotional, and how words, images and personal interpretation can work together to move you to new feelings.

Storytelling's own story is an epic one stretching back through time, across lost continents and diverse cultures, yet timeless principles may always be found at work in the most engaging stories. These principles represent clues to understanding story's power of communication.

We have opened the book by outlining the twenty key principles we use as a creative toolkit for effective storytelling. They are followed by 32 stories written and illustrated to bring these stories to life.

Finally we look at the business of story. Great storytellers understand how story works for them. This book is about unlocking and sharing the power of story with you.

We hope this book will take you on a journey.

Remember the greatest story may be the one you've never told.

The Twenty Principles of Storytelling

The twenty principles we have outlined are grouped into five areas that we feel are critical to successful engagement . They range from 'First Principles' that are associated with establishing a compelling storyline through to more executional aspects such as dialogue and exposition that are grouped under 'Craft'.

1.

Stories are questions not answers.
Controlling ideas are loaded. They may take the form of questions, invitations, visions or challenges. But the one thing they all have in common is their ability to grab our attention. They are the central idea that everything hangs off. But very rarely do they give us all the answers.

2.

What's at stake? The premise lives at the heart of a great story - what it's really about. By experimenting with the meaning of a story you can, in turn, change 'what's at stake' for the audience. A great premise taps into a unifying need or truth and is a great start point for pro-actively managing engagement.

3.

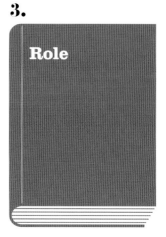

All the world's a stage. One of the great secrets of storytelling is to make sure you give the audience a role. We do this by providing opportunities for people to play their part in our world. It's critical that the story is 'handed over' so that it can take on new life in their world.

4.

Using the dark side of story.
Most stories we love revolve around a protagonist struggling against forces of antagonism. What you fight against defines what you stand for. It explains why you exist in the world and what you want to change for the better.

5.

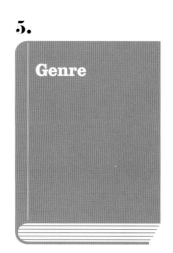

Playing with expectations. In almost every story, there are dominant genres at play that the audience is expecting. By challenging traditional thinking with alternative, surprising genres you can often unlock fresh ideas

6.

Setting

Where am I? Our job is to create an enticing world that people want to step into. We do this by defining the fundamentals such as geography, time and place then allow the audience's imagination to do the rest in line with archetypes.

7.

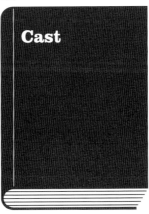

Cast

Character reveals character. Cast can be used to reveal information about the story world, raise tensions and much more. Sometimes it will be necessary to adapt the cast to heighten engagement or reveal something new.

8.

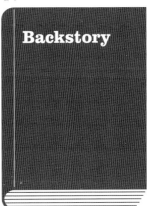

Backstory

Walking backwards for answers. Backstory is often used to add depth and colour to characters and plots. But, just as importantly backstory can provide 'reasons to believe' which all audiences crave.

9.

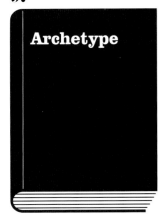

Archetype

There's a hero in all of us. Authoring the roles that characters play is a creative exercise that holds great potential for indentifying new opportunities for engagement. If you don't author a role with clarity and conviction the likelihood is that your audience will do it for you and your character will lose its impact.

10.

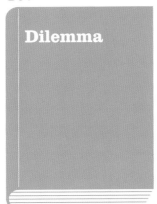

Dilemma

True character is revealed under pressure. People like to know what a character is really made of before believing in them. So our advice is to find ways of proving yourself. A hero's journey is littered with obstacles.

11.

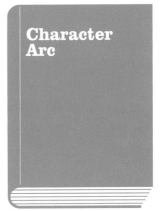

Character Arc

To thine own self be true. To create empathy a character must face inner and outer change and test their desire and commitment to win our hearts. The change in character from beginning to end is known as the 'character arc'.

12.

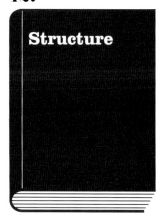

Bringing stories to life. Structure is about organising story events with engagement in mind. The approach centres on plotting activity to see climaxes, identify gaps in engagement and foreseeing issues that must be addressed in advance to ensure the story satisfies throughout.

13.

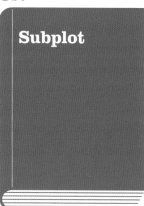

Weaving the story together. Subplots are invaluable for dramatising a point, highlighting contradictions and exploring big themes. They are a common objective of heightening engagement in the central story.

14.

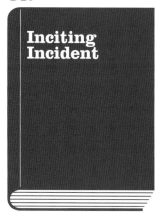

Start with a bang. This principle is specifically designed to change story direction and force re-appraisal. An inciting incident stops us in our tracks and makes sure there is no going back. From this point on, everything will change.

15.

Give them what they want. Humans are blessed with the ability to predict what might happen next. Indeed, trying to figure out twists, turns and climaxes is one of the most enjoyable experiences for an audience.

16.

What was that noise? Audiences love the great unknown. They seek new experiences, heightened emotions, dark mysteries and startling revelations. We may maximise engagement by allowing our story to unfold with dramatic revelation (as opposed to simply telling it).

17.

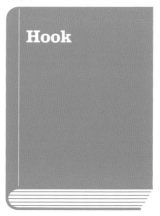

Point of View

Walking the line. There's always more than one side to a story. Exploring alternative points of view is one of the best ways to see a familiar story with fresh eyes. It can reveal more compelling angles and insights for developing new opportunities.

18.

Hook

Making stories irresistible. Hooks have become increasingly important in such a fast, cluttered world in drawing the audience in. In fact, nowadays, stories start before the beginning with hooks.

19.

Exposition

Show not tell. The power of story is subtle. It dramatises so that the audience can see, hear and feel things. Actions almost always speak louder than words.

20.

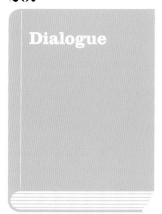

Dialogue

Use the force. Dialogue is the result of hundreds of decisions around character, motivation, backstory, casting, intention and can transform character and story. In an increasingly two way world, dialogue and its mastery are critical.

RAC—

She Waits
A Story of Stories

CONTEXT

The simple image of a woman observed on a street in New York City is open to any number of suggestions and back stories that can bring an unknown character to life and make us engage with her situation.

PRINCIPLES AT PLAY

SHE WAITS

and waits and waits. .

It's 7.30pm, she's opposite the coffee shop on 13th, the coffee shop she's seen him in every weekday morning for eleven years. Today she finally asked him out on a date. She hasn't got the wrong place and time. He doesn't show. She'll be there for another hour until pride drags her home. She will remember the ferry ride forever. Bought a quart of vodka and sipped it from a bag. Never going to know what happened to Alvin from Mani's...

She waits for her husband and their son. Her son is taking them out for dinner for the first time. He is eighteen. He is nervous of course. He is going to come out tonight. She has known for years. Her husband will spit his food out, but he will accept it and even raise a glass to him. They will drive home laughing. Their son will sleep well tonight...

She waits for a phone call. She hopes to be told that she has got the job in Seattle. She has wanted this for two years. She has worked tirelessly and deserves it but she's convinced herself they will say no to avoid disappointment. She tries to sound calm. The moment she knows, she shrieks, shouts and does a little dance, those passing will crane their necks and wonder...

She waits for news of her mother. It won't be good...

She waits for her daughter outside the track. Her daughter is a star in the athletics team. She drives her here every day at 5.30 am. She doesn't like to be with the other parents. It's her time. She comes out here for a cigarette and a think. She listens to Motown. Her daughter will appear, as she does every day, tired and ravenous. She will hand her breakfast and drive her to school...

She waits for her dealer. She owes him a grand, she's desperate, she's sick and she's running out of reality. It's spinning out of control. Her black eye will force the issue, she has to tell her family. Will this be one of the best days of her life...?

Bread
A Generational Story

CONTEXT

A visual idea for a dream and the ambiguities of what it could reveal about a central character at the heart of this story.

PRINCIPLES AT PLAY

BREAD

Every day, in a small room on the Upper West Side of Manhattan, a man lay down to rest in the afternoon and had the same dream in black and white. He would see himself on a summer day standing in a crystal clear stream, with tall oak trees lining its banks. As the clear water flowed past, a beautiful fish swam around his legs before slowly swimming away. He always awoke serene and refreshed, after exactly half an hour.

Olivier Charbit had moved to New York from Rouen, with his parents when he was five years old. In 1937 his father opened a boulangerie on the Upper West Side, on 72nd between Columbus and Amsterdam. For years it was the best-kept baking secret on the island. Its traditional French baguette, baked twice a day, tasted and felt like real French bread. An orderly queue formed outside the bakery early in the morning and in the middle of the afternoon. Restaurants served Charbit's bread. It was delivered to the best addresses. The small bakery constantly ran at full capacity. Olivier worked hard, but it never crossed his mind to expand the business. His goals were typical of every parent, he wanted his children to succeed, to go forward in life and fulfil their ambitions, whatever they might be. He concentrated on just two things: providing a secure life for his family and baking.

Olivier Charbit never changed. His bread was a simple mixture of yeast, flour, water, salt and sugar. He saw himself as the guardian of his father's memory and his secret recipe. Steeped in traditional values, he was a man of ritual. Every morning, at 3am, he rose and prepared the first batch of dough. At 7am, when the first bake was complete, he took bread to his family's small apartment upstairs and breakfasted with them. He returned to his bakery as the shop opened at 8am. After a simple lunch upstairs, again, he returned to prepare the second batch of bread. At 3pm, whilst it was in the oven, he went to his little office and napped on a camp bed for exactly half an hour.

One day, he went for his nap and never woke up. His wife found him with the most serene look on his face, which was of great comfort to his family.

Olivier had a son Jack and a daughter Cécile, while she had fulfilled all her father's hopes and become a doctor, Jack misunderstood his father's aspirations for him. He had discovered the underbelly of New York at a young age and had spent most of his life arguing with his father about getting work and qualifications. He had drifted from one dead end job to another, dropped his friends in the neighbourhood and rejected the community and its values, which meant everything to Olivier.

After his father's death, Jack was angry and annoyed that his hand had been forced to take over the bakery, but his mother and sister helped him find his feet and slowly but surely Jack discovered he had a natural talent. The queues once again formed outside Charbit's Bakery. Jack grasped success with open arms and expanded the business. Soon there were four more Charbit's Bakeries in Manhattan and Jack ensured all their bread was every bit as good as the first baguette made at his father's and grandfather's shop.

Strangely, Jack never went into the little office, where his father had taken his daily nap, until what would have been Olivier's 80th birthday. At 3pm that day, Jack lay on the old camp bed and he, too, dreamt of the summer day, the trees and the fish in the crystal clear stream. He awoke refreshed and with a serene look on his face.

Today, the neighbourhood still keeps many small family businesses that go way back. The florist, the butcher, the deli, the electrical store, the shoe store, the bistro are all run by first and second-generation immigrants with a proud heritage of family and tradition. The original Charbit Bakery is still there and its owner, Jack Charbit, is a man of ritual.

TITLE

The Last Kings of London
A Modern Story

CONTEXT

This started as a simple observation of a piece of tradition that is dying out. Storytelling allows us to embellish this to embrace more universal themes such as tribalism and belonging, which go much wider than the subject matter.

PRINCIPLES AT PLAY

THE LAST OF LO

"You've got to be born into it or married into it, there's nothing more London than a Pearly."

KINGS
NDON

Johnny is a Pearly Prince, he'll be King one day. He spent today shaking a collecting tin in Covent Garden. Originally, each London Borough had a Pearly King plus one for the City of Westminster and one for the City of London. Dedicated to the church of St. Martin in the Fields, Pearlies collect money for charity.

"Nowadays, there's about forty of us families that carry on the tradition. Originally we were costermongers who wore flash boy outfits to stand out in the market, then an orphan named Henry Croft sewed all these buttons on his clothes and that's how the tradition started. Costers always looked after their own, but Henry wanted to help other orphans."

They shake the tin and collect the metal. They do invaluable work. Johnny goes to Covent Garden every Sunday to do his bit. He's got the walk, he has. Got a bit of a swagger. Tourists love the Pearlies.

"I like to chat with them. They love my London accent. We have a laugh, pose for photographs. We're relics really."

The tourists call them cockneys not Pearlies. To them they are London icons. Johnny shows me the designs on his outfit. Thousands of buttons adorn his jacket.

"My Dad was crowned in '82. King of Camden, that's where my family are from, they sold fruit and veg from a market stall. My Mum sewed on all the mother

of pearl. They came from her mother and father, who were Pearlies themselves. All the later ones are plastic. Mother of pearl is way too expensive now. My girlfriend sews them on these days.

The horseshoe is for luck, the dove is for peace and the donkey cart is the symbol of the costermongers."

Johnny has a son but he's not keen on becoming a Pearly.

"He wants to do his own thing now. He is busy at weekends. Tradition doesn't mean as much anymore."

Johnny fears the Pearlies will disappear.

"A museum rang last week to ask for outfits and stories. It felt a bit weird talking to them, like we were an endangered species."

I met Johnny on a train. It was a Sunday and he had finished collecting an hour or two before. After a while I asked him why he was on a train heading out of London. I had assumed that he was going to an event somewhere.

"I'm going home, mate. We live in Milton Keynes now. We left London five years ago. My family can't afford to live there anymore."

The Truth About Barry
A Story of Belonging

CONTEXT

Characterisation and setting paint a backdrop of an apparently distinct world that allows us perspective on our own behaviour.

PRINCIPLES AT PLAY

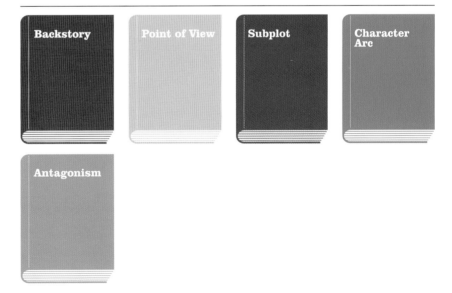

THE TRUTH ABOUT...

●●●*Barry* had always been big. Ever since he could remember, people would speculate about Barry's size. Maybe he had big bones. Perhaps he had a thyroid problem or a slow metabolism? But Barry had always known that he just ate too much.

Doughboy, they called him at school. Fat Barry Ashworth never a member of any team, never part of any gang, most things were off limits. The swimming pool was out of bounds, Barry not being too good at floating. Mr. Jeffers, the maths teacher, said it was the perfect example of The Archimedes Principle. At school sports day, Barry showed the parents where to park and ate biscuits while the speeches were being given. He never won a prize. Barry's only achievement was Grade 1 double bass, but it went unnoticed given that Barry was the only boy deemed big enough to hold the thing upright at such a young age. The boys laughed, the girls laughed, even the teachers laughed, happy to deflect their eyes from their own shortcomings. Being fat in the 1970s was no easy thing.

Such was Barry's life. He had no real hobbies. As the other boys came to terms with their sexuality, so Barry came to terms with the loveless lot that was his life. His parents waited patiently for Barry to excel at something, anything, but by his late teens it became apparent that he was unlikely to be an achiever in any field. But, despite Barry's impediment, there was one blessing. Barry never complained. He never even told his parents about the taunts and the bullying.

When pressed to find a positive about Barry people would comment on his eyes. Barry's eyes sparkled and seemed to do all of Barry's talking for him. It would be true to say that Barry had smiling eyes... great big smiling eyes.

Whilst others went on to higher education, Barry left school at the earliest opportunity and sought a career in solitude. He became an electrician. He had no electrical skills and was not particularly good with his hands, he felt safe as an electrician. Barry was on call twenty-four hours a day but most of his work was done between 9 am and 5 pm, Barry liked it that way.

Each day his job would be different and would require all of Barry's concentration and diligence. His big fingers had trouble with small circuit boards and wires, but, fed tea and biscuits, Barry applied himself manfully, always smiling, always courteous, knowing the end of the day was getting nearer.

Barry was a creature of habit. When the day was done, he parked his blue van outside his house, or as near as traffic allowed and prepared his evening meal. There was only ever one for dinner but, even so, the house was immaculate. Barry was not a bad cook. Admittedly, his repertoire was limited, but Barry enjoyed most things he prepared, especially spaghetti bolognese. Dinner for one, food for ten.

Plate and pans cleaned and put away, Barry would shower and change from his blue overalls to jeans and T-shirt. Even though his outfit seemed lacking in warmth for winter, Barry felt at his most comfortable in it.

As soon as he was changed, he would leave the house and take up position at the bar in his local pub. Same place every day, seven days a week.

Barry drank mild ale, always had done, man and boy. When he arrived in the pub, they would pour his first pint without saying a word and Barry would nod his appreciation, paying them with exactly the right change. Everyone knew who Barry was in the bar, but he never spoke to them, just smiled with his big brown eyes. Sometimes he would help the bargirls by changing the loo roll in the gents or bringing the sign in from outside at closing time, always with the minimum of fuss. It was the way Barry liked to live his life. He paid his bills and respects in equal measure and asked for nothing. If anyone noticed anything about Barry, apart from his larger than average frame, then it was those eyes.

Behind those eyes, in Barry's world, he wasn't thinner or better looking. He was just happy. Given that Barry spent virtually all his life in his world, not ours, then Barry was always happy, hence the smiling eyes.

You see, a long time ago Barry had realised that there was not much for him in the real world, so he had just gone right ahead and invented his own. Barry had developed the art of non-verbal communication. Talking just got in the way.

In Barry's world, people came to visit. People hung on his every word. He was articulate but a good listener, funny but not overbearing and a great raconteur. He had many friends and was fond of all of them. He remembered all their birthdays and was always there for them when they needed him. He was rarely selfish and admonished himself when he was. He wasn't perfect and he had always known that.

Tonight was a special night. He had promised to take Jasmine dancing. As he supped on his second pint, he picked up on his thoughts. Jasmine was beautiful. She was a model and had been on the cover of many a magazine. We might have thought Jasmine too flirty and flighty, but she was perfect for Barry. He had forgotten that Jasmine couldn't dance, or so she said, as he led her out onto the floor. She soon got the hang of it and they laughed and danced until the lights went up. She felt comfortable with Barry. Who wouldn't?

By the time Barry came to, it was drinking up time. He felt light as a feather as he left the pub.

At the speed the car was going, there was nothing much the driver could do. Barry was a pretty big target and he was hit broadside at a touch over forty miles an hour.

A small crowd gathered around a motionless Barry as a crimson pool formed around his head.

Some people might have survived the accident but if the truth were told, Barry grasped death as others would have grasped life. Barry leant over towards Jasmine and pulled her towards him. He kissed her with all the passion that 25 years of solitude could muster. Barry smiled.

• • •

A Table for Three
A Mystery Story

CONTEXT

In this genre character and intrigue can be built up quickly at the beginning of a story, the smallest details having the potential to carry the most information. We are forced to interrogate each detail to extract the most meaning and are hooked into following what comes next to discover the outcome.

PRINCIPLES AT PLAY

A TABLE FOR THREE

EXT. NEW YORK CITY. NIGHT

January 6th 1952. The city is in the middle of Arctic weather. As the sequence ends the camera roams the streets and we see frozen slush piled high on the sidewalks. A man tries to walk across the street glistening with ice whilst keeping his footing. The city seems quiet as everyone shelters from the cold.

CUT TO:

INT. RESTAURANT. EVENING.

8pm and the buzz, by contrast, is deafening. The air is full of New York chatter and smoke. A waiter hurriedly brings a whisky to table 13, the corner table by the window of this traditional brasserie on the Upper East Side. The waiter serves the tumbler of Chivas and a small jug of water. He strikes a match and reaches out to light the cigarette of **BLEECHER CORNELL**, an immaculately dressed gentleman in his early forties. Bleecher is well known here but tonight he looks a little agitated and wipes his forehead with his napkin. Facing a wall mirror, he straightens his bow tie and his dinner jacket lapels. He is alone at his table which heightens our sense of his importance.

WAITER: Are you three tonight Mr. Cornell?

BLEECHER: What does it look like to you?

The waiter shines through the comment as we see the three chairs.

WAITER: Very well Sir. Shall I get you the menu?
                 Can I get you something to get you started?

BLEECHER: Hold the menu until my guests arrive and get
                 me some of those stuffed green olives.

WAITER: Yes sir.

BLEECHER: And a phone.

The waiter is on his way.

WAITER: On its way Mr. Cornell, sir.

Bleecher takes a big slug of the viscous liquid and looks out onto the frozen street. Seated at another table a big man stares at Bleecher whilst the rest of his party make conversation and eat steak tartare, loudly.

                                                        CUT TO:
INT.APARTMENT.SAME
A middle aged man in his fifties lies on a light coloured carpet with his throat freshly slit. His crimson blood empties his body at a steady rate and has already dyed his dress shirt. The man is wearing a dinner suit and heavy coat and was obviously about to leave when the attack happened.
The camera pulls back to reveal a sumptuous uptown apartment. In the half light, someone opens the door and leaves. **CU**. on the hands of a woman. A beautiful sapphire ring on her finger. The phone starts to ring.

                                                        CUT TO:
INT.RESTAURANT.SAME
Bleecher is sweating slightly and smoking another Lucky Strike. He is listening to the earpiece of a telephone that has been brought to the table.

                                                        CUT TO:
INT.CORRIDOR.SAME
A beautiful woman in her thirties, MIRIAM LOVALL enters an elevator in an upmarket apartment building. She is exquisitely dressed and holds a mink coat in her arms. A young couple in the elevator admire the sapphire necklace that she wears. It is locked in place with a sterling silver tiger clasp. She holds herself beautifully and looks calm and radiant.

                                                        CUT TO:
INT.RESTAURANT.SAME
Bleecher slugs Chivas and picks at some olives. The man at the other table continues to watch Bleecher. Bleecher suddenly turns

and catches his eye as if aware he'd been watched for sometime. Bleecher's look withers.

CUT TO:

EXT.STREET.SAME

Miriam walks across the street and something catches her attention. She looks up and smiles.

CUT TO:

INT.RESTAURANT.SAME

Bleecher sees Miriam walking across the street towards the restaurant. As she steps off the sidewalk a car arrives at speed and knocks her down. She is thrown onto the hood and the car carries on without stopping. Her body lies on the side of the road, blood trickles from the corner of her mouth and stains the snow. There is no sapphire necklace there anymore.

Everyone at the restaurant has heard the accident and they press up against the windows to watch the action. Bleecher watches Miriam's still body. He shows nothing.

He slowly takes a slug of Chivas and waves to the waiter. If anything, he seems calmer than before despite events. He looks around the restaurant and takes in all the faces. No one is looking at him. All eyes are on Miriam's dead body, even those of the guy at the other table. A distracted waiter arrives.

BLEECHER: Check please?

WAITER: Oh, sure, you're not eating?

BLEECHER: Not anymore. Something's come up.

WAITER: Oh
               (*checking for the total*)
               That's a dollar fifty please.

Bleecher hands him a five and goes to get up. The waiter starts to look for change.

BLEECHER: Keep it.

WAITER: You sure, Mister Cornell?

BLEECHER: I'm sure.

Bleecher heads for the door past the big guy who is too busy staring at Miriam to notice.

CUT TO:

EXT.RESTAURANT.SAME

Bleecher hits the sidewalk. He hails a taxi and gets in without even glancing at the body in the road.

TITLES ROLL

The Shirt
An Open-Ended Story

CONTEXT

This is a story that makes the viewer co-author. The words lead their thoughts.

PRINCIPLES AT PLAY

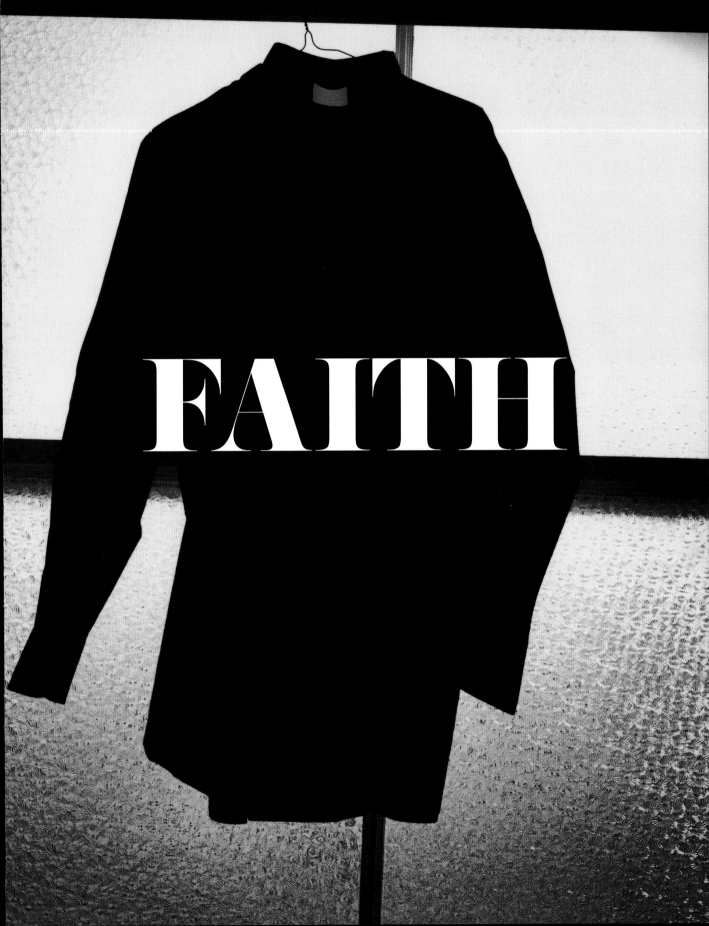

L'Hirondelle
A Story of Freedom

CONTEXT

Changing a point of view and setting can dramatise a singular emotion. The genre here frees the storyteller to play with that emotion.

PRINCIPLES AT PLAY

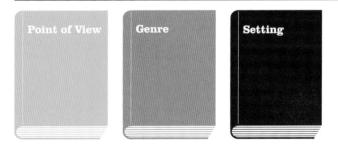

Now I see you darting there
High above I pick you out, clear as day
In the dazzling sun you come and go, come and go

I love you hirondelle, I love your buzz, your yes and how
you will not stop in midday heat, be slowed down or miss a beat

You see it all and move so quick
While the sun just sits and stares

I hear you sing
    You sing so loud
Want us all to hear

                    How very different looking down
        So many souls of sombre brown

            That whole sky seems made for you
    Eating up its vibrant blue
                I want to fly with you
                    beautiful hirondelle

EPISODE

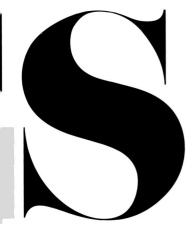

Notes From Within
A Story of Hope

Finding an unexpected outside point of view can change the perspective of a story and help resolve a dilemma.

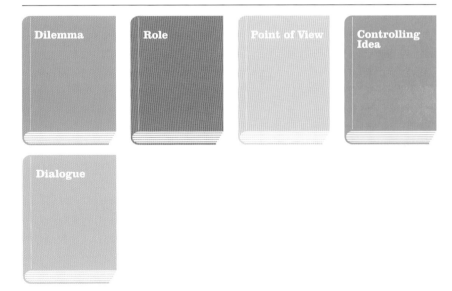

NOTES FROM WITHIN

I want you both to remember how much it takes to be this happy.
I want you both to promise never to take that for granted.

I want you to think about how good life is together, so you can see
how much it needs protecting and how powerful you can be as
two, rather than two ones. It's rare. You won't find it everywhere.

You must never grow so comfortable that you forget what
uncomfortable feels like.

You must never assume, or believe, there are greener meadows
or better days in some other place.

And when I am born and old enough, and you both are older still,
you can look at me, your child, and remember the glorious lives
that a simple love can bring.

Father Christmas
A Story of Giving

A family episode, which depicts an everyday hero in a modern context.

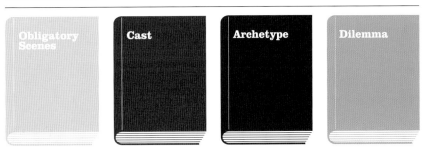

FATHER CHRISTMAS

———————

It was December 25th. I was nine years old and had been excited about Christmas ever since I opened the first window of the Advent calendar. We took turns the four of us, first me, then my three elder sisters. At night I would sit for hours by myself, cross-legged, in front of the illuminated Christmas tree, guarding the presents and watching the pile grow. The tree never had new ornaments. They were all familiar, each one had a history.

That room, all lit up, still seems so perfect to me. Every now and then my Mum came in to pour herself sherry. She seemed happy in December and her breath smelt sweet for the whole month. She played a vinyl L.P. of carols sung by King's College choristers, left on repeat. She constantly hummed along. I never got bored of it.

Finally, Christmas Day had arrived. We had opened our stockings, raced through breakfast and were about to open the presents under the tree. Then the phone rang. Someone at the docks, said Mum as she passed the phone to Dad. Three Chinese merchant sailors whose boat had just docked all had chronic toothache. My Dad was a dedicated dentist. He put on his coat and left. Someone had popped our balloon. It was like one team not coming out of the tunnel on to the pitch on Cup Final Day.

My Dad was managing director of Christmas in my house. It fell to pieces without his leadership. He smiled all day, he handed out the presents and always remembered to put batteries in the toys and carved the turkey. Without him, Christmas just stopped. We waited and waited. All twenty-four hours of Christmas were ticking past. He even missed the Queen's Speech on TV. Mum tried her best to keep our spirits up, but she was in the same boat as us. She was missing the star of our family show.

Then suddenly, when we were beginning to give up, Dad came home. He had four Chinese pears in a bag, one for each of us children, and a Chinese lantern for Mum. We were so glad to have him back, we ran round like mad things, showing him stuff, asking him a million questions. I remember him picking me up. His coat was freezing cold, his face was colder. He smiled in that moment and that smile will always be Christmas for me.

Olympic Dreams
A Story of Sacrifice

CONTEXT

A strong premise is created when so much is at stake, so much to lose.

PRINCIPLES AT PLAY

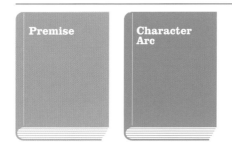

Monday November 4th

Robbie Renwick- Placed 8th (*LAST!*) in 200m freestyle Beijing final 1:47. 47

Michael Phelps – Placed 1st (*new WR!*) in 200m freestyle Beijing final 1:42.96

Mark Spitz – Placed 1st (*new WR*) in 200m freestyle Munich '72 final 1:52.78

My personal best – 1:50.03

JESUS!
I'm nearly three seconds quicker than a world legend and about ten seconds slower than the Olympic champion. Exhilarating and depressing.
Crave pizza!

Wednesday November 6th

Freezing this morning at 5 am Mum looked tired. I want to take her breakfast in bed and then go to bed myself...forever.

They all had a brilliant time at Wendy's party. It ended at 7 am. Said I didn't care. *I cared!*

Want to tell Mum that I want to give up, but it would mean all those early mornings, all those weekends, all that driving and sandwich making and Dad earning extra money would be wasted. Look at Lewis Hamilton's dad how much he sacrificed. Now he's got a big watch and lots of cash. I'll try to carry on.

Sunday December 12th
NEW PERSONAL BEST! 1:49.94

In the 49s! Would put me in different world ranking wise. I feel spurred on. Want to celebrate. Eat a lot of chocolate in service station when I nipped to loo. Mum none the wiser. When I drop seven more seconds, Phelps will be in trouble.

Wednesday February 10th

Want to lie on sofa, play Playstation and go to bed late. My PB has not been beaten. I am a county swimmer. I won't win the Olympics. I don't think I want it enough. I see the others at training. They think I'm great but that's just at our pool. When I go to events, I get to see the others. I'm not as big. My arms and legs are like twigs compared to some. They're developing into *GIANTS!* Sub 1:49 seems a long way away and even that's not good enough. I'm working so hard in the gym and not getting anywhere. I feel shit, shit, shit. If my coach saw this he'd make me read The Secret in a padded room.

Saturday February 25th

Went to party. Got drunk. Really, really drunk. Missed training. Mum loses it with me, crying. Think she knows deep down. We end up hugging. I love her so much for everything she's done for me. We lie on her bed and watch old black and white film and she lets me eat rubbish. *Heaven.*

Monday March 3rd

4.30 a.m. This has to stop. Mum was up to make me breakfast. It's ok if I'm going to win Gold and Mum gets the big watch, big house, but two boys swam sub 1:49 last week. I haven't come close.

Sunday March 20th

Came 5th. Long drive home. Listen to iPod to hide from Mum and Dad.

Monday March 21st

My Dad goes to see my coach. I will not be competing in the 2012 London games and I will not be competing for my county any more. Dad comes home and gives me a hug. He tells me I haven't let anyone down. *I know I have.*

The important thing is winning not taking part
London 2012

I'm Fucking Angry
A Story About Issues

I saw this dog at a funfair in Paris. If you use humour, you can convey threatening or frightening messages which would otherwise be rejected.

PRINCIPLES AT PLAY

I'M FUCKING ANGRY

The Law of Physics
A Story of Revelation

A story may centre on a moment of transformation, which changes the protagonist's journey forever.

*THE
LAWS
OF
PHYSICS

IT WAS A MONDAY AFTERNOON LATE IN DECEMBER, I'M SURE OF THAT. THE DAMP, MISTY AIR BIT DOWN AFTER THE WARMTH OF THE RESTAURANT. THE COLLEGE SPIRES WERE SILHOUETTED AS DUSK FELL OVER CAMBRIDGE.

We had been out for a Christmas lunch and I was slightly drunk. My dizzying undergraduate ego was full of ideas and the arrogance of youth. I wince now at the thought. I was trying to impress a girl, from Corpus Christi, and Clive, a Cambridge tutor.

He looked impassive as we passed by.

"Homeless or a tramp?"
Clive said vaguely before we fell into earshot.

"Oh, tramp sounds so old fashioned in that context,"
laughed the girl.

I laughed too. I suppose it was Christmas carelessness that came across as cockiness. Bonhomie stripped of innocence.

"Would you like a pound?"
I asked, a little too loudly, stating the obvious.

"That would be nice,"
he said.

"What are you going to sing for us?"

"I'm not a performer,"
he replied.

I remember distinctly, at this point, shifting onto my back foot.

"Well you've got to do something for the pound."
I paused.

"Everyone does something for the money."

He made me feel uneasy. The tutor headed off with the girl. I heard them giggling, when they'd gained some yards, and I knew that I had provided the humour.

The tramp stayed silent. I suddenly felt sober and shivered.

"Ask me a question?" he said.

"For the pound," he added, in case I'd forgotten in my drunkenness.

"What subject?"

"Any you like."

"What about physics?"

"Physics will be fine."

"For the pound?"

"For the pound."

Physics was my subject. I was a physics scholar. I asked him the question. It was short but involved. As the first syllable left my mouth, I could hear voices in my head saying, "You can't ask that, even you don't know the answer." I was showing off. It was shameful really.

I noticed he had a dog, a black Cairn terrier, which had started to go grey. My gaze shifted to it. I couldn't look at him. I knew he knew. The pound was his. His answer was instant, No prevarication, No possibility that he was wrong. I understood he didn't even see the question as a tough one. His engine was idling in first gear, second at the most.

His answer left me with a thousand questions . The tramp was a pound richer.
I didn't know it then, but I was much wiser.

Come What May
A Story of Friendship

This scene is taken from the second act of a screenplay. This is the inciting incident from which there is definitely no going back. From now on, things will never be the same again for Debbie or May. This forms the basis for the rest of the story, namely how two friends deal with this event and how their friendship and actions will change their lives forever. Inciting incident is seldom something wonderful and if it is, it is well hidden at the time.

PRINCIPLES AT PLAY

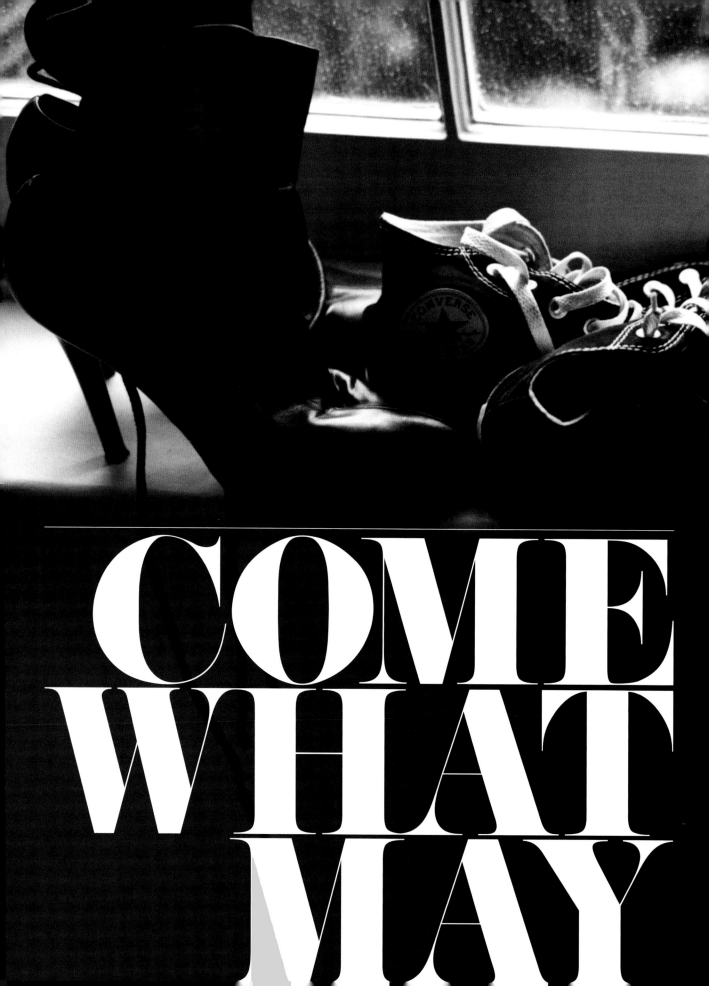

COME WHAT MAY

INT.DEBBIE'S APARTMENT.NIGHT
A track blares out of the stereo as May dances to it, dressed up in Debbie's clothes.
The doorbell goes. May goes to the intercom, obviously thinking that it's Debbie

MAY
Oh, you're back are you?
Just in time for the party.

May carries on even more frenzied dancing. We see someone push the door open which is ajar. It's the **CITY GUY** from before. He leans on the door jamb looking mighty pleased with himself. Suited and booted with a king sized twitch, he is dripping in slime. May carries on until she recognises him in the mirror. She stops with a jolt and turns off the music.

CITY GUY
Oh dear, have I missed the party?
Don't stop on my account.

MAY
I thought you were...

CITY GUY
Well, I'm not am I? You dance with Saphire, don't you Roxy?

MAY
Erm, yeah, I do. Did you come to see Debbie?

City Guy moves into the room. May looks defenceless.

CITY GUY
No hurry! Why don't you give me a dance darling.

MAY
Sorry?

City Guy starts to move towards her

CITY GUY
Go on, a little private dance for yours truly. Then we can have a little party.

MAY
No thanks!

Debbie appears in the background. City Guy turns to face her.

DEBBIE
And what the fuck do you think you're doing here?

CITY GUY
Always a warm welcome. Just came along to get the party started.

DEBBIE
Fuck off!

CITY GUY
Oh dear! Well you won't mind settling the bill then, will you?

DEBBIE
I'll pay you next week, just fuck off and leave us alone.

CITY GUY
Not what you said last week is it? Well, let me see. Perhaps I'll take a grand now as a sign of good faith and collect the rest next week. How does that sound Saphire?

He runs his finger over the furniture. Debbie rummages frantically in her bag. May stands looking like a small girl dressed in her mum's clothes.

CITY GUY (CONT'D)
It's a lovely place you've got here Saphire, sorry, Debbie.

Debbie squashes a bundle of notes into his fist.

DEBBIE
Here's two hundred. It's all I've got at the moment.

He smiles as he walks towards the door. Then he stops and laughs.

CITY GUY
There is an easier way honey!

DEBBIE
Fuck off!

He leaves. Debbie just stands there with May looking at her imploringly for what seems like an age.

CUT TO:

INT.DEBBIE'S LIVING ROOM.NIGHT
May lies on the sofa. She lies next to Debbie who has her arm protectively around her. Debbie suddenly looks exposed and tired.

DEBBIE
I'm so sorry.

MAY
How long?

DEBBIE
A year....maybe more.

MAY
How much?

DEBBIE
Five grand.

May rolls over to face her.

MAY
Oh Debbie....

Debbie hugs her.

" I'VE BEEN SENTENCED TO LIFE BY THE KHARMA POLICE! "

DEBBIE
I know. May, I might have fucked up and slept with the wrong people but I'm not a slag, I'm not! Time to face my demons I reckon.

MAY
It'll get better. I promise you.

DEBBIE
Not before it's got a lot worse.

They lie in silence.

CUT TO:

INT.A TOILET.DAY TWO WEEKS LATER
Under the cubicle doors, we can clearly see two sets of feet. One pair are encased in six inch perspex stilettoes, a gold G string straining around her ankles. The other feet are wearing Converse and a pair of battered jeans pulled down around her ankles. The silence is deafening. Only their feet twitch. Voices come forth from behind the cubicle doors.

DEBBIE
Oh, bollocks! (a beat). May!

MAY (O.C.)
Oh, crumbs!

DEBBIE (O.C.)
You're kidding?

MAY (O.C.)
No!.

They both appear from the cubicles and the camera jibs up to meet them. Both are carrying pregnancy tester strips . They make their way to the sinks and mirrors, Debbie looking radically under dressed compared to May.

DEBBIE
You couldn't make it up could you? I do not

bloody believe this. I've been sentenced to life by the kharma police!

They both hold their testers to the light. May reads the instructions on the box at the same time. Debbie spies this out of one eye.

DEBBIE (CONT'D)
What colour do they go again?

MAY
Blue.

Debbie looks hard.

DEBBIE
Bollocks!

May looks at hers. It's blue, no doubt.

MAY
We could check again.

DEBBIE
Yeah! Fourth time lucky eh? May, we are up the duff love, no doubt about it.

MAY
Debbie?

DEBBIE
What?

MAY
Who do you think is the....

DEBBIE
Don't even go there. What about you? The world's most fertile woman. That's one off immaculate that is. Come on, you're late as it is. We'll talk about this after work.

The door opens and SOPHIE bursts in. The girls rapidly hide the testers.

SOPHIE
Debbie, Alfie's looking for you.

May picks up her bag and goes to leave.

MAY
Busy out there?

SOPHIE
Usual suspects.

DEBBIE
Go on, shake a leg. We'll talk later. (whispers) It'll be fine, I promise.

May hurries out of the toilet.

My House Crumbles
A Story of Life

A house, or another external object, can serve as a device to represent a character's rite of passage.

PRINCIPLES AT PLAY

MY HOUSE CRUMBLES

This is my house. It's falling down. I know that. It needs a new start, an overhaul. It needs gutting to be honest and that's a task I'm not up to. Don't get me wrong, I'm as house proud as anyone, but there's only so much you can do, so much you can give. It started with the peeling paintwork, worn edges to the carpets.

It's just me living here now. I rattle around only using a couple of rooms. They seem bigger, colder and harder to heat. There are some rooms I've not been in for years. They'll be damp and needing attention, but I just keep the doors shut.

It took us years to get the garden the way we wanted. So much effort to just manage nature, but now it has taken over again, encroaching all the time.

In the morning, when I wake up, I feel the damp in the air. It has a musky smell. I can feel it on the sheets. The damp is in the joists, which means it's everywhere.

When we moved in there were smells of new paint and soft leather. In the evening the scent of jasmine came through the open sash windows. Now, of course, they don't even open any more, they are jammed.

The house used to be full of smells and people and things: laughter, smoke, history, seasons, songs and parties, Christmas, washing up. Young and old, all at once, all mixed up.

The memories run from room to room, slamming doors and running down the stairs. They make me smile. They make this house worthwhile. They warm it up for a moment, you know what I mean. It's beautiful then.

I read magazines sometimes and see new things. They look wonderful, fresh. There's a young couple next door, just starting out. It looks different in there, very new, bright and clean. It's just the same as this house really, but it's got a future.

This is my home, you see, but I'm leaving soon.

Love In the City
A Love Story

CONTEXT

A fashion love story which allows a poem to weave its way through the photography, giving it narrative, back story and character.

PRINCIPLES AT PLAY

LOVE IN THE CITY

skips a beat
where spirits meet
on this sunny street

this is the biggest deal
the best scene
that there's ever been

we are going to play it out
shout it out
for real

suddenly the sidewalk's clear
there's no one here
anymore

it's time to be aware
of everywhere
every tiny thing
could well mean everything

extract, distill, reduce once more
We are left with something pure

who could ask for more?

right now

In this city.

STOR
TELL

Y–
ERS

How Tall Stories Came to Be
A Children's Story

CONTEXT

A children's fantasy story can explore a universally negative theme acceptably, with humour to make its point and present a central character with more wisdom than would muster credence in reality.

PRINCIPLES AT PLAY

HOW TALL STORIES CAME TO BE

A LONG TIME AGO, in a land far away, lived a King and a Queen. They were very happy and had an enormous family of seventeen children. The King and Queen loved each and every one of them with all their hearts but, there was just one problem all the children were girls and the King wanted a son very much. Finally, the King's wish was granted and a son was born. They named him Sam and the whole nation celebrated.

The King wanted Sam to be wise and learned so that one day he might rule the Kingdom, justly.

As soon as the Prince was old enough, the King set to work telling him the history of their Kingdom and its people. He used the same stories which his own father had told him many years before.

Soon the King realised that the storytelling was starting to take up all his time. He sent out his men to find the wisest men in the Kingdom whom he believed would provide a priceless source of knowledge and understanding for the young Prince.

Every day the Prince was visited by different story tellers

and teachers. He would learn of famous citizens and their noble deeds. He would listen to accounts of heroic battles with wily beasts. He would hear of achievements and setbacks, victories and defeats, for the King believed that he should understand both good and bad.

Before he went to bed the Prince would tell the King what he had learnt. The King loved to listen as the Prince recounted the day's revelations.

One day the Prince came to the King wearing a particularly wide smile. The King asked what had made him smile so. The Prince told the story of a land far away across the sea, where the more you ate, the faster time passed. In this land the houses were made of chocolate and the roads were paved with caramel. It rained custard and when the grass grew it was made from long pieces of mint liquorice. Indeed, the lakes were full of warm custard and the boats were made from biscuits.

The Prince implored the King at the end of the story. *"Can we go and see the custard lakes?"* *"No, we can't, not today,"* said the King. He wanted to give himself time to think. He kissed the Prince goodnight. The King slept little, turning the story over in his mind, and his mouth watered slightly when he thought of the caramel roads.

In the morning the King summoned the storyteller, a huge man, who was over ten foot tall. The King asked him why he had lied to the Prince. The storyteller told him that sometimes he exaggerated details to make a point. In this case, the story was meant to teach that all actions have their consequences and all things should be done in moderation. With the constant temptation of their candy surroundings, the citizens of this strange land had to restrict their greed.

The King found himself liking the storyteller very much. He was, however, worried that his son would still believe that this land of chocolate and caramel really existed.

The King and the storyteller discussed this problem for a long time and they sweetened their dilemma with just a little chocolate and caramel, taken in moderation.

The next day, the storyteller and the King sat in front of the Prince with wide smiles on their faces and little smears of chocolate around their mouths.

The Prince looked excited and asked, *"Tell me more about the land of liquorice grass and custard lakes."*

*"*Before the story starts today, I want to explain something,*"* said the King. *"The story that this gentleman told you, from now on, is to be called a tall story in accordance with the stature of this noble gentleman. A tall story contains facts that may not be true but are there to highlight a lesson. Every time you see this very tall gentleman, or indeed any tall storyteller, they will tell you an excellent tale that carries within it an important lesson, which will make you much wiser and prepare you for life as a King one day."*

The King left his young son with the storyteller. In the corridor outside was a long queue of very tall gentlemen, each with their own stories to tell.

The Last House in London
A Story of Fear

Storytelling allows us to roadtest emotions. Magical and foreboding worlds full of incredulous characters and situations allow children and adults to experience fear and excitement, without ever putting them in danger.

PRINCIPLES AT PLAY

Antagonism Setting Genre

THE LAST HOUSE IN LONDON

This was the view from my bedroom as I grew up. Ours was the last house on the road, which was the last road on the estate, which was the furthest estate from the town. My father called it the last house in London. We liked that.

As children, the forest was our enchanted playground, a great big theatre set where we would look for a new story every day. We as good as lived among the trees during the holiday months and at weekends, but as soon as the sun started to go down and the shadows from the trees lengthened, we were back in the house, quick as you like. My father saw to that. He told my elder brothers Arthur and Elliot to take care I followed them home and they would call me, "Tabitha, Tabitha," if I strayed too far away in the forest.

My father was the great instigator of stories; he lit the blue touch-paper of our young imaginations and sketched out the fictitious characters, who inhabited the forest and our world. From the tree stump of an old oak, my father conjured up heroes and villains. From the overweight general with sabre and white moustache to the wisest owl in the world, who could tell the time without a watch, and always knew when it was time for bed.

We would sit rapt as he told his tales. He talked of an Italian soprano who had lost her voice but the birds could still hear her. "She's singing Rigoletto," my father would say, stopping quite suddenly. We'd stop in our tracks and listen, hardly breathing. "I can't hear anything except for the birds," Arthur would say. "Exactly," said Dad. "They love Rigoletto."

There were crocodiles with no teeth and an army of blue ants, who lived on honey. The list was endless, the images rich, colourful, lustrous. Dad wrote the prologue and we filled in the missing pages.

Sometimes my father arrived home from work after we'd gone to bed. He always came to our rooms before we went to sleep and asked us about our day. I'd say we had met the general and he talked for hours about the battle on the Nile. My father, embellishing, would ask me to send the general his warmest regards the next time I saw him. These were intoxicating words. I dreamed of staying late in the forest to meet the general's friends, perhaps even his daughter.

One day Elliot asked about a noise we all heard, a ferocious whooshing sound that came from the trees. My father looked concerned. He paused, then asked, "Are you sure you want to know?"

As we sat on the oak stump, my father began his story. "Long ago, as the tale goes, there was a beautiful white house on the other side of the forest. A wealthy merchant lived there with his wife and their daughter, Hermione. She was an only child, indulged by her devoted parents. She wanted for nothing.

One day she was playing in the forest and her father was called away to attend to some business. Hermione asked if she could stay on alone and play. 'You may Hermione, as long as you are home before sundown.' Hermione continued to play and forgetting her father's request, she stayed in the forest too long. When the sun went down that evening, Hermione did not return. Her father went to the spot where he had left her and started to call her name. He stayed there, believing, hoping she would come back to him. I wish there was a happy ending, but there wasn't. She never returned. They say that the noise you can hear is her father calling. They say if you listen closely, it's unmistakable, H-e-r-m-i-o-n-e, H-e-r-m-i-o-n-e."

My father got up and left. We listened to the wind for a few seconds, then I think it was me who screamed and we all sprinted after him.

We never once stayed long enough in the forest to see the darkness descend on the trees.

Early Morning Train
A Story of Provenance

No matter how far you travel from home, your earliest lessons are the ones that never leave you.

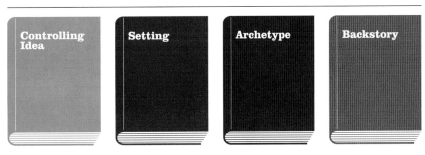

EARLY MORNING TRAIN

I'm on a train, rushing home to see Grandad...

"I HAVE DONE WELL FOR MYSELF."

I have done well for myself. I sit up front in first class, my legs stretched out. I smile smugly, leaning my head on the cold windowpane. Grandad laughs at me whenever I tell him. "All that money for a bigger seat! It's the same bloody view, Son, train gets there at the same time." Always referred to me as Son. If anyone else called me Son, I'd bristle. The train sails quietly over the rails, through the dawn light towards my home.

I remember Grandad sitting in his allotment, talking on the bench outside his shed, rolling a cigarette, his big, gnarled, hardworking hands creating gentle precision. Grandad wore the same boots on the allotment for thirty odd years. They matched his hands: cracked, weathered, industrial. Grandad used to cook at the allotment too, in a big pot on a brazier, potatoes and cabbage straight from the ground, served with butter.

His allotment was centre stage in that community of gardeners. He was a leader. Not only did he win rosettes for his tomatoes and the like, but his attention to detail,

"HE HAS NEVER ASKED TO SEE ME BEFORE."

his gardening tips, worldly wisdom on rootstocks, motorbikes and foreign policy made him a sage, politician, diplomat and elder. Everyone listened to him. They saw him work, fight to protect his values and keep his word, Grandad had earned respect.

In that small cosmos I learnt it all from a man who had never entered a boardroom but played the game better than I ever hoped to do.

Grandad may be gone soon. That is the nature of succession. He has never asked to see me before. Whatever happens, life goes on. It makes me feel closer to him and appreciate his little cosmos in a small village in the North East of England.

I want to learn more.

Hurry train, hurry.

My Whisky Lullaby
A Story of Perception

CONTEXT

Sometimes it falls to a third person narrator to unravel layers of character and give us the details of narrative that make a mini tragedy work.

PRINCIPLES AT PLAY

MY WHISKY LULLABY

Jimmy is pretty much the first person you see when you get inside the Cross Quays bar.

He is almost certainly the first you hear. Perched on one of the old bar stools, he's almost the only authentic thing left in this old docklands bar these days.

In the heyday of industry, the pub was open round the clock to accommodate the thirsty shift workers. Original is the word they use to describe it today. Colourful describes best the way it used to be. Not many of the regulars now look familiar with manual labour. What would the dockers of yesterday make of the soft furnishings and lunch menu? People come here now to learn something of the area when they move here. They need to colour in the gaps so they can justify their decision to live in the middle of nowhere.

They say that you used to be able to buy pretty much anything from the back door of the Cross Quays if you

> "A WALK ON THE WILD SIDE."

had the cash and were feeling courageous. Hard drugs, a gun, prescription pills, a sofa, a left-hand drive car. You would simply put in your order with the right person and it would eventually make its way to the Cross Quays from somewhere in the world. On Friday lunchtimes there were strippers. A pound in the pint pot got you more than you bargained for, according to retired dockers. Going to the Cross Quays was a coming of age thing. A walk on the wild side.

Jimmy is a shade under six feet tall and seventeen stone. He is a heavy man. His hair is cropped short under a woollen cap. His nose is a little too big for his face and his teeth look like a bag of chips. He wears a big donkey jacket, whatever the weather, and he has his drink and a box of matches laid out in front of him on the bar. They are his props.

Jimmy tells stories in return for drink. Jimmy roots the pub back to its reason for being. He is the storyteller, the tour guide to life in the docks with the rosiest tinted spectacles in town. Jimmy drinks single malt if someone else is paying, but something much cheaper the odd time he has to buy himself.

> "JIMMY WAS NEVER ABLE TO HOLD DOWN A JOB AGAIN."

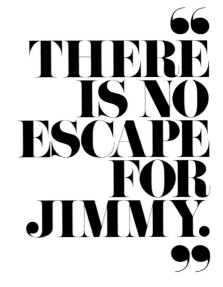

"THERE IS NO ESCAPE FOR JIMMY."

There are two distinct audiences for Jimmy. There's the lunchtime crowd and the evening drinkers. At lunch Jimmy is sober, well Jimmy isn't drunk. He tells of the tall ships that used to crowd the river. There are the stories about his grandfather, a merchant seaman who brought home a monkey for his mother and pineapples and pomegranates years before the rest of us tasted them. He remembers the soldiers, who waited to go to war, and the aristocracy, who used to board the transatlantic liners. He describes the luxury of silks and spices from India and the tragedy of stowaways and near starvation during the strikes. How they all helped each other out in hard times, one big family. His audience are wide-eyed and full of questions.

Then there's the evening crowd. Jimmy is a little drunk by now and is prone to anger and exaggeration. The crowd want to hear of the arguments resolved with bare knuckles. There are black marketeers and shadowy characters refined and sharpened by Jimmy over the years. They hunger for tales of legendary three day drinking binges and womanising. Jimmy never disappoints and fine tunes expertly for his audience.

There's one tale Jimmy tells that interests me more than any other. It's his version of the Queen's Silver Jubilee street party in 1977. His version for the lunchtime crowd is "roll out the barrel" and a raucous but endearing East End knees-up that went long into the night. For the evening crowd, however, it is a tale of engaging debauchery, of stolen kisses with friends' spouses, of skinny-dipping in the river and wild excess. I've heard both and they are beautifully told slices of history loaded with golden images. But I've also heard the truth.

In 1977, the docks were full of the unemployed, and on the night of the Silver Jubilee Jimmy and his friends got drunk here. Jimmy ended up in hospital for a month, beaten senseless by a man named Tan for saying something out of turn. A costly mistake as Jimmy was never able to hold a job down again.

Tan features in all of Jimmy's stories as his old friend. I wonder why he seeks Tan's friendship so long after their argument and I wonder how the crowd would react if they knew the truth.

Every night, when I polish the glasses at closing time, I see the sorrow in Jimmy's eyes. I see an alcoholic trying to escape but each night becoming a little bit more bound up. There is no escape for Jimmy. This is the only world he's got.

I Plunge
A Dark Story

This story was just pure emotion and representative of changing moods. Genre can facilitate this quite brilliantly.

PRINCIPLES AT PLAY

I PLUNGE

———————

Under mongrel skies that bark and snarl,
Whip vicious winds that cool my skin.

Shadow and the light play on a crystal day,
Under the surface of which

I plunge.

Going deeper now, collecting things that slow me down.
Surface many miles from where I came.
This journey never stops,

I know.

Break the shiny top,
The pebble skims along
Aware of complex things underneath.

Choices have been made and I am on my way.
Packed my bags today

and

I'm gone.

———————

MED
STOR

Want Me?
A Story of Desire

Brands are stories, well told.

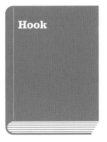

WANT ME?

I am pure and clean. I can answer your needs I won't change your life.

I am a rational solution to your problem. I will quench your thirst. I am at hand. I am enough. More than enough. Go on, drink me, consume me. Look at me for God's sake!

I'm not enough for you. I know that. I need a story. Oh, how I yearn for a story

You want more. A beautiful story in which you can believe, be a part of, belong to. Say with a shiny badge held high that you've made the right choice. It's a story you can find independently and feel like you're a pioneer. Part of the advance party that finds me. My story will feel like one that reflects yours. You will tell my story to others, embellished of course and they too will feel like they have discovered something new. You won't for a minute think that my story has found. you.

You are that kind of person. You want emotion. You want provenance, a delicious back story that gives me geographical roots and history, since 1958. A story that connects you somehow to somewhere sublime, to a better life.

My story may be about how I come from deep inside the earth and am filtered upwards through the foothills of the Himalayas, under intense pressure, to appear as a spring 15,000 feet above sea level. Maybe I was discovered by a mountaineer and drunk for the first time looking at the most incredible view after an incredible achievement, My story may be about intensity, otherworldliness and may have a hint of spirituality. My story may be about the best discoveries being the purest. My story may well imply you may not be ready for me. My story will urge you towards your own discoveries and achievements. Sounds good enough to queue for. Bet that'll quench your thirst for something. My story will be about overcoming obstacles and ultimate redemption. My story will sell water.

You'll want sumptuous packaging that delivers me in the most innovative way. You want to be shown who drinks me and aspire to that person, connect with them and all they stand for, you may even want to look like them. You want far more than is logical. You'll want

a trick or two. A special delivery spout perhaps or a new me that 's two degrees cooler. Much cooler.

You'll watch my story come to life in adverts sixty seconds long that are memorable for their black and white silence. You'll want to see some famous name drinking me on the streets of New York in the middle of a heatwave. My special spout will be invaluable then. You'll see it's me even when the famous person has their hand over my million pound logo. You'll want to see my name in lights, want me to sponsor a TV show and have a website. You'll hear the word of mouth come around to you in a great big circle of storytelling. You'll want it all.

You want a story that you feel a part of. You want to be the hero in that story. The star. You want a brand. That's what you really want. If I were a brand then you would desire me. You'd want me then.

But not right now.
I'm just a bottle of water.
•••

Pomodoro
A Story of Unity

A short film script which started life as an idea for a TV commercial. The examination of family relationships are the ingredients for a recipe for life.

PRINCIPLES AT PLAY

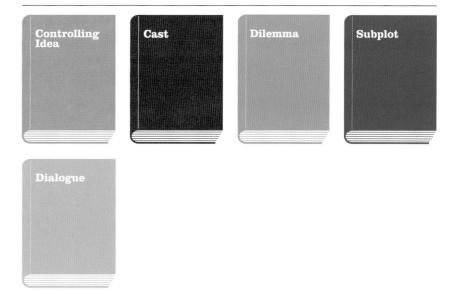

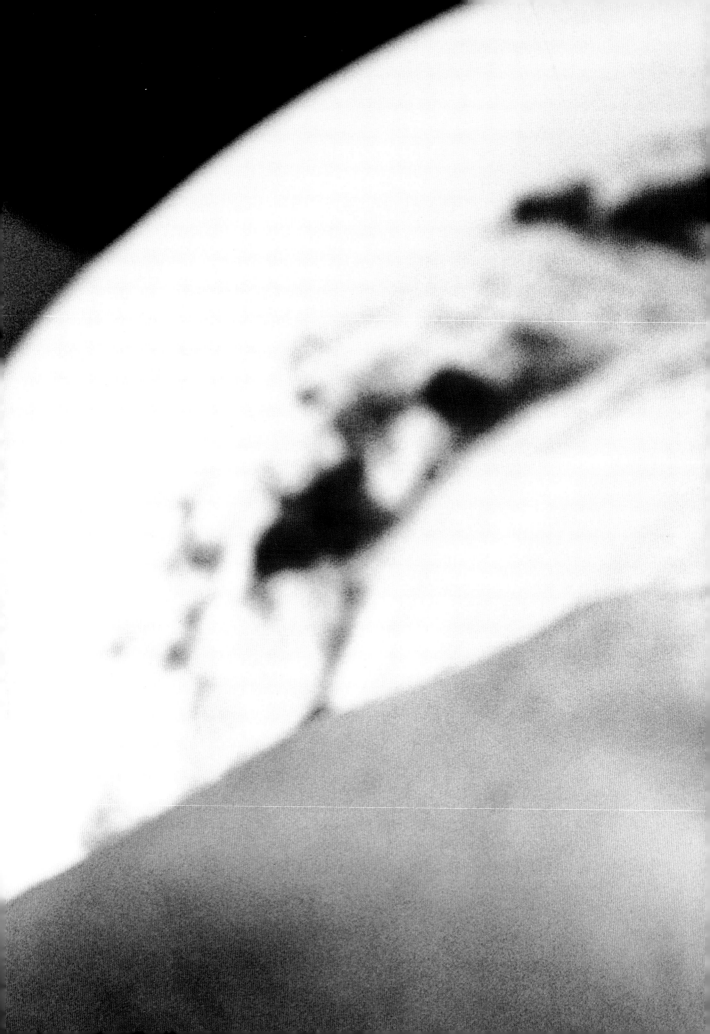

POMODORO (A TALE OF A TOMATO SAUCE)
BY
SIMON ABOUD

INT.KITCHEN.DAY

TITLES ROLL:
A huge pan of beautiful, red, unctuous, bubbling
sauce sings on the kitchen range. It is stirred,
loved, coaxed into life as some freshly ripped
basil is thrown in. It becomes mesmeric.

                    V.O.
          (a young Italian male) So, this is
          a tale of tomato sauce. I mean, (a
          beat) what could more be simple?

A ladle transfers the red elixir from the pan to
a large bowl of freshly boiled angel hair pasta and
then the bowl is picked up by a young waitress and
taken to a table of hungry Los Angelians. The place
is simple, classic and full of people and chatter.
What we notice most is the noise, like a giant
heated debate. The bowl is placed in the centre of
a plainly laid table of white linen and china and
is clearly a "family" portion. The waitress fills
four bowls with the angel hair pomodoro. The table
looks on in wonder, eyes full of expectation. As
soon as the last spoonful is served, they are upon
the food like vultures, sprinkling on the Parmesan
and pepper. The food halts the chatter, only for
a moment mind.

                 WAITRESS
          (above the din) Enjoy.

She walks back to the station and to the maitre'd,
an elegant woman who evidently rules the roost.
This is ANGELA. She moves around the restaurant,
meeting, greeting. People like to know Angela at
Otranto. They like Angela to know them by name.
It says something about them. Angela approaches
a table where a well known and debonair English
actor, LAURENCE NICE, holds court with three
beautiful women and his agent. Onlookers gawp,
point iPhones in his direction and slurp tomato
sauce. Laurence has a napkin tucked in around his
neck and his face is covered in pomodoro. He is
thrilled to see Angela.

                  LAURENCE
          Angela. You look radiant. I missed
          you.

                  ANGELA
          (unfussed) Thank you Laurence.
          And how are you this evening? It's
          good to have you back.

                    LAURENCE
          (looks at the ladies who nibble)
          We, Angela, are splendid. Simply
          splendid. This is the first time
          here for the girls. Very exciting.
          Pomodoro virgins no less.

                    ANGELA
          Well, we are very pleased to have
          you here ladies. Laurence is one
          of our most regular guests and we
          would welcome any friend of his
          with open arms. How was the shoot?

                    LAURENCE
          Arduousness, punctuated by moments
          of Italian divinity.

The agent explains to the ladies.

                    AGENT
          Laurence had Otranto Fed Ex
          Pomodoro sauce to him in Mexico.
          Daily.

                    ANGELA
          Ten litres a week no less.

                    LAURENCE
          (smiling) Hungry crew. A little
          home from home Angela. It earths
          me. Everyone loves your beautiful
          food. You should expand Angela,
          expansion is the key. The world is
          waiting for you. They're ready to
          (takes a big old slurp) slurp you
          right up.

There are streaks of tomato sauce down the sides
of his face like flames. One of the girls slowly
leans into shot and licks a little from his face.

                    GIRL 1
          (her face lights up) It's
          delicious.

                    LAURENCE
          Told you so. Bloody nectar. Where's
          Jackie Junior?

                    ANGELA
          Out and about. You've got to stop
          filling his head with crazy dreams

Laurence. He's young and easily
swayed by someone such as yourself.

                    LAURENCE
I shan't Angela. I simply shan't.

                    ANGELA
Enjoy your meals.

                    LAURENCE
Oh I will, just you watch me!

He winks at her. Angela moves off. Laurence kisses
one of the girls and covers her face in sauce.

                    ANGELA (V.O.)
The sauce is what we are about.
Otranto is built on a river of
pomodoro, beautiful, red pomodoro.
It's basic, fundamental, goes back
to when we started, where we
started, and that was a while ago.

We see that most tables have a large bowl of angel
hair pomodoro on them. The crowd is mixed, old and
young, families, media types.

                    ANGELA (CONT'D)
It's 75 per cent of what we sell.
It sends Jackie a bit nuts
sometimes, sees it as a slight on
the rest of the menu, which is very
good I'll have you know. Jackie
Senior and me say that. They love
something that's the main thing and
they pay handsomely for it which is
a nice profit. We'll take some of
that.

Angela goes to another table of four where only
three sit.

                    ANGELA (CONT'D)
Hey Dossalina, where's Johnny got
to?

                    DOSSALINA
Dead is where Johnny has got to.

Angela puts her hand over her mouth. We see that on
Johnny's empty seat is a framed photo of Johnny.

                    ANGELA
When? How?

Dossalina puts her hand over her heart and taps it.

                    DOSSALINA
     A week ago.

The table raise a glass to Johnny's chair.

                  DOSSALINA (CONT'D)
     He wouldn't miss dinner for
     anything less.

                     ANGELA
     They'll always be a chair for him
     here.

They kiss.

                                    CUT TO:
INT.KITCHEN.DAY
JACKIE, Angela's husband comes from the serving
pass bearing more angel hair pomodoro. He looks
stressed as he serves.

                  ANGELA (V.O.)
     I say to Jackie, we'd be a heap
     more stressed if the place were
     empty. Jackie runs on stress
     though. I think that comes with
     inheriting something though. The
     responsibility.

                                      CUT TO:
EXT.CAR PARK.SAME
The car park is packed. We see the neon sign. It
reads "Otranto Since Approximately 1906". We see a
couple get out of a Bronco, Arizona plates.

                  ANGELA (V.O.)
     It's a pretty popular place, news
     gets around.

The couple pass another couple leaving with a big
doggy bag.

                  ANGELA (CONT'D)
     Some folks order an extra portion
     for their imaginary friends and
     then take it home to freeze it. You
     know, to recreate the experience at
     home at a later date. Jackie
     doesn't like that, Jackie senior,
     on the other hand, says it helps

                    spread the gospel...amen to that.

                                                    CUT TO:

EXT.CAR PARK.LATER
The last car rolls out of the car par. The kids in
the back hold doggy bags and have tomato sauce
around their mouths.

                                                    CUT TO:

INT.OTRANTO.SAME
Angela Z's the till, the roll is long and
impressive. She whistles as Jackie walks past with
a big plate of angel hair pomodoro.

                    JACKIE
          And? (referring to the till roll)

                    ANGELA
          It's certainly not to be sniffed at
          Jackie. The numbers are good.

They kiss and Jackie goes to sit in a booth by the
window as a young girl THEA clears up around him.

                    JACKIE
          You were great tonight Thea,
          magnificent.

          THEA
          Oh, shut up dad and eat.

He smiles and starts eating.

                    JACKIE (V.O.)
          Table 5. We always eat at table 5.
          It's where my father eats and it's
          where his grandfather Jackie ate
          when he started the restaurant.
          It's kind of tradiitonal.

We cut to Jackie's POV and see girls leaving the
strip bar next door. He waves.

                    JACKIE(V.O.) (CONT'D)
          The Scallinis have always been
          a naturally inquisitive family.

He looks back and catches Angela's eye. She's got
the measure of him. He smiles and takes another
mouthful of the pasta.

                    JACKIE (CONT'D)
          Hey Eddie (towards kitchen) I think
          the sauce is even better than usual

                                    tonight. What did you do, put the
                                    basil in a little later?

                                                              CUT TO:

INT.RESTAURANT.DAY
JACKIE SENIOR sits at table 5 with his wife SUNNY
who knits a scarf. Craggy, Italian and wearing a
white hat, plaid seersucker pants and huge
sunglasses, he talks to camera.

                    JACKIE SENIOR
               It was my grandfather Jackie who
               started the meatball rolling way
               back in the day.

Sunny rolls her eyes.

                    JACKIE SENIOR (CONT'D)
               He came over on the boat round
               about 1906. Nobody seems to know
               for sure.

                         SUNNY
               Nobody including your grandfather.

                    JACKIE SENIOR
               Ay ay ay. What do you know? A woman
               who knits a scarf when it's 38
               degrees. Ay ay ay. Let the man rest
               in peace.

                         SUNNY
               Come on and get on with your story.

At that moment Thea arrives with a bowl of angel
hair pomodoro for Sunny.

                    SUNNY (CONT'D)
               Thank you Thea my darling.

                         THEA
               A pleasure grandma.

                    JACKIE SENIOR
               What's with the interruptions?

                         SUNNY
               Get on with it!

                    JACKIE SENIOR
               Have you thought maybe I'd like a
               bowl of pasta? Has anyone thought
               about that?

                         THEA
             When you've finished your story
             grandpa.

                    JACKIE SENIOR
             Ay, ay, ay. I don't want to hear no
             slurping Sunny.

She waves a knitting needle at him with a mouth
full of pasta.

                  JACKIE SENIOR (CONT'D)
             So it turns out that Jackie, Jackie
             senior senior senior, brings very
             little with him on his trip to the
             New World. A small bag of clothes
             and some wine and cheeese from
             Otranto, his hometown near Lecce
             back in Puglia. His father gave him
             a few bottles of good robust
             Primitivo, you know in case he gets
             invited to dinner or something. Now
             that's a long journey to New York
             and Jackie has a couple of glasses
             on the boat ride if you know what I
             mean. In fact, when he arrived the
             only thing he had on him was the
             last remaining bottle of Primitivo,
             even his bag of clothes had been
             stolen.

                         SUNNY
             Lost in a card game.

He just curls his lip at her.

                    JACKIE SENIOR
             This obviously meant the Port
             Authority were struck with a
             strange sight, my grandfather in
             his bare feet, offering them a
             glass of wine.

                         SUNNY
             Drunken bum. It's amazing that the
             man ever got past Ellis Island.
             A miracle. Couldn't string two
             words together apparently and them
             customs officers thinking he was
             speaking some fancy Italian
             dialect.

                    JACKIE SENIOR

                    Ay ay ay. Eat your pasta and tone
                    it down woman.

                                                  CUT TO:
INT.RESTAURANT.DAY
Angela and Jackie sit in booth number 5 with their
daughter Thea. Jackie picks up where Jackie senior
has left off.

                         JACKIE
                    So Jackie arrives in his bare feet
                    and it's November. He sobers up
                    pretty quick in minus 5 and
                    hotfoots it to The Waldorf where he
                    hears there's jobs for eager young
                    Italian boys as kitchen porters. So
                    he starts there, all innocent,
                    never having been further than
                    Lecce. The New World beckons, the
                    door is slightly ajar.

He looks at Angela like this is a routine they've
got going.

                         ANGELA
                    And that's where the legend of the
                    sauce begins.

                         JACKIE
                    Yeah, you tell it better than me.

                         ANGELA
                    So there's a lot of staff at The
                    Waldorf don't you know, and when it
                    came to feeding themselves, they
                    couldn't order their staff meals
                    off the menu. That would costs them
                    a fortune so a different sous chef
                    every day had the job of cooking,
                    very cheaply, I may add, for
                    hundreds of waiters, cleaners, bell
                    hops and the like. And every day.

                                                  CUT TO:
INT.RESTAURANT.DAY

                         JACKIE SENIOR
                    Every single day, it was a thin
                    grey vegetable soup with a piece of
                    bread. And what with Jackie
                    cleaning lobster and steak off the
                    fancy china plates for a living.
                    Can you imagine?

INT.RESTAURANT.DAY

                    ANGELA
          So one day Jackie asks a sous chef
          if he could make the staff meal.
          Well, the sous chef is thrilled.
          Knowing he could only use
          vegetables, Jackie opens up the
          remaining bottle of Primitivo and
          makes a big pan of Pomodoro just
          like his mum back in Otranto and
          binds it into angel hair. Simple as
          that.

Jackie and Thea nod.

                    JACKIE
          Simple as that. The legend is born.

                                        CUT TO:

INT.RESTAURANT.DAY

                    JACKIE SENIOR
          They can't get enough of Jackie's
          sauce and the staff demand Jackie
          makes it every day. They go mad for
          the stuff. They're baying for it
          like dogs. Various sous chefs try
          to emulate the sauce but they can't
          get close...still can't (laughs)
          and soon Jackie's angel hair
          pomodoro comes to the attention of
          the head chef at the Waldorf
          Astoria New York City no less.

                                        CUT TO:

INT.RESTAURANT.DAY

                    THEA
          And they offer my great great
          grandfather a job in the kitchen
          and, not only that, they want to
          put his angel hair pomodoro on the
          menu.

                                        CUT TO:

INT.RESTAURANT.DAY

                    JACKIE SENIOR
          Imagine that. Ay ay ay.

INT.RESTAURANT.DAY

                    ANGELA
          But he says no. Imagine that. At 19
          years old he turns down chance of
          a lifetime because of two things
          1) he has realised the power of the
          pomodoro and 2) maybe more
          importantly, his feet were still
          cold and he heard that Los Angeles
          was warm all year round. So he
          comes cross country and trains at
          The Beverly Hills Hotel for four
          years until he got financed by a
          famous film producer called Lou
          Bronstein who apparently ate the
          angel hair pomodoro every single
          day.

                    JACKIE
          Jackie just honed and perfected the
          sauce and Lou brought in the
          business until Otranto was known
          all over town for the food and the
          buzz. And that recipe has been
          handed down generation to
          generation.

Angela shakes her head slightly.

                                        CUT TO:

INT.RESTAURANT.DAY

                    JACKIE SENIOR
          I'm telling you it's like Coca
          fucking Cola.

                    SUNNY
          Jackie, watch your tongue!

                    JACKIE SENIOR
          It's closely guarded, it's unique.
          It's fucking unique.

Sunny goes to scold him.

                    JACKIE SENIOR (CONT'D)
          Just knit woman.

                                        CUT TO:

EXT.FREEWAY.DAY
A young good looking man mid twenties drives a

vintage Alfa. He wears shades, talks into his
phone. He's got the whole thing down.

                                        CUT TO:

INT.RESTAURANT.DAY

                    JACKIE
          What makes it unique?

                    ANGELA
          Where do you start? You want the
          right tomatoes and you want them
          peeled when they've been boiled.
          Got to be in season mind. You never
          want a mealy tomato.

Pull back to reveal the whole family are around
table 5 eating the angel hair pomodoro before
service starts. A TV plays Italian soccer out by
the kitchen.

                    JACKIE SENIOR
          It's about getting the consistency
          right, bringing the ingredients
          under control.

                    SUNNY
          And never ever let the garlic burn.

                    JACKIE
          Oh no, nor the onions. There's
          always a temptation to let them
          blacken a little.

                    ANGELA
          Season it nice right at the get go.
          Generous salt and pepper.

          JACKIE SENIOR
          And don't be shy with the wine.
          What wine? Now that would be
          telling. But like I say, Otranto
          pomodoro, now that's special, the
          crown fucking jewels.

                    SUNNY
          Watch your mouth Jackie!

                    JACKIE SENIOR
          Ay ay ay! (waves her away and dabs
          a tear with his hankie)

                                        CUT TO:
INT.CONFERENCE ROOM.DAY
We see through a glass wall into a packed
conference room. The good looking kid from the car
is at the head of the table. A smart looking woman
presents to the kid and the gathered suits. The kid
holds court, very cool.

                                        CUT TO:
INT.RESTAURANT.DAY

                    JACKIE SENIOR
                Over a century we've been making
                this sauce. If my grandfather
                knew..

He bangs his fist on the table, the sauce is spilt.
Angela goes to console him. Thea wipes up the sauce
with a finger and then puts it in her mouth.

                    ANGELA
                Don't Jackie...we know.

                    JACKIE
                What the fuck does he think he's
                playing at?

                    JACKIE (CONT'D)
                He's just a boy pa.

Thea rolls her eyes.

                    ANGELA
                He's our son Jackie. (a beat) and
                he has dreams.

                    JACKIE SENIOR
                Dreams! (a beat) is that what you
                call this act of betrayal Angela?
                Is it?

They are silent except for the sound of Sunny
knitting and the football on the TV. The crowd
cheer.

                                        CUT TO:
INT.SUPERMARKET.DAY
A shopper pushes her trolley along an aisle and
stops to observe something closer. We pull back to
reveal a giant pyramid of cans. "Otranto Extra
Special Pomodoro Since Approximately 1906". The

woman picks up two tins and throws them in her
trolley. Next to the tins is a giant display of
angel hair pasta. A poster shows the perfect
serving suggestion in the familiar looking bowl
which is also on sale. The whole Otranto package is
available.

The woman pushes on past a food display where
promotions people dressed Italian are sampling the
product to eager shoppers.

                                        CUT TO:
INT.APARTMENT.DAY
An African American family are sitting to eat
dinner. Mum brings out the main attraction, a giant
bowl of Otranto angel hair pomodoro. The family are
excited and await their serving. As DAD is served
his dinner he notices something on the TV.

                        DAD
            Look kids, it's your favourite.

We zoom into the TV over the food laden table,
where a commercial has just started. In the ad,
it's Laurence who plays Jackie and Angela's son
looking identical to him and speaking with a strong
Italian accent. He walks into shot in an empty
restaurant looking super slick, a regular young
Marlon Brando. He turns to camera as he sits at a
table which is surrounded by a cast that looks
incredibly similar to Jackie Junior's family,
there's a Jackie Senior, a knitting Sunny, a
Jackie, an Angela and a Thea, all slight
caricatures of the real McCoys.

                        LAURENCE
            So what makes Otranto pomodoro
            sauce unique?

A freshly made bowl of angel hair pomodoro is laid
in front of the family.

                    LAURENCE (CONT'D)
            Is it the fresh tomatoes?

                        ANGELA ACTOR
            Is it the gently fried garlic
            and onions?

She takes a mouthful.

                        JACKIE ACTOR
            The fresh herbs?

He tucks in.

                    JACKIE SENIOR ACTOR
          Or the distinctive taste of the
          wine from back home in Puglia?

He takes a slurp of the wine.

                    THEA ACTOR
          Or is it the secret recipe that's
          been in the family from
          approximately 1906 when my great
          great grandfather first made his
          Pomodoro Sauce.

Suddenly the mood changes,

                    SUNNY ACTOR
          Oh, so no one's thought to give the
          old lady a bowl?

                    JACKIE SENIOR ACTOR
          Maybe the old lady's had enough if
          she knows what I mean?

                    ANGELA ACTOR
          Now that's not on, take that back.

                    JACKIE ACTOR
          Pa! What's with the fat stuff
          already? We could talk about the
          sound your teeth made if we had
          no dignity!

                    JACKIE SENIOR ACTOR
          Ay ay ay! You're not too old for
          a clip on the ear young man.

                    JACKIE ACTOR
          Too old and too quick grandad. Go
          suck your teeth.

The conversation boils over. Laurence turns to
camera

                    LAURENCE
          But what makes Otranto pomodoro
          sauce so special? Well that's easy.

He turns and looks at his faux family, as he does
we see him turn the tin of sauce around to read
"Scallini's Pomodoro Famiglia".

                    LAURENCE (CONT'D)
          Take all the ingredients of your
          family and put them all at the

                    table, serve and stand well back.
                    Each one of them will bring
                    something unique and...I promise
                    you a different experience each and
                    every time. It's been keeping
                    Otranto restaurant busy for over
                    100 years, it's great sauce for
                    heated conversation.

Laurence hugs the Jackie Senior actor.

                    JACKIE SENIOR ACTOR
                Get off me will you! AY ay ay.

We cut to a shot of the beautiful bubbling sauce on
the range.

                    LAURENCE (V.O.)
                Otranto Pomodoro Famiglia.

Cut back to the faux family and their heated
conversation

                    LAURENCE(V.O.) (CONT'D)
                    Better altogether.

                                              CUT TO:

INT.RESTAURANT.DAY
The family have just seen the advert on the TV by
the kitchen for the first time. They are speechless.

                    JACKIE SENIOR
                Ay ay ay.

                                              CUT TO:

INT.APARTMENT.DAY
The youngest of the African American family looks
at her dad. She wears glasses and has a moutful of
pasta.

                    YOUNG GIRL
                Ay ay ay.

                                              CUT TO:

EXT.RESTAURANT.DAY

Jackie Junior pulls up outside the restaurant and
parks the Alfa. In the passenger seat is Laurence,
cool as a cucumber in his shades. Jackie Junior
steps out. His family stare at him through the
glass from table 5. We can see they have a lot to
say to him.

                    END

Sate
A Story of Greed

The controlling idea is a place where men are reduced to nothing more than animals. The ironic setting is the fictitious "Sate", the most expensive restaurant in the world.

29/06 **SATE**

- Access by helicopter only! $3,000 before you eat a morsel
- Helicopters buzz in hanging like angry flies in the sky
- Fly in rich - fly out poorer (in many many ways)

1st IMPRESSION - Sheer size of crowd
INTENSE NOISE
Fall of the Roman Empire, fin de siede. All this money, no civility
Noone worries about carbon footprint here. Rare food u guzzled without a thought for the cost
Drink Petrus by the case, here ($20,000 a case) who cares?!

Bloated, red eyed diners, faces smeared with the vestiges of their indulgence
Served by reptilian waiters who outnumber them ~

On the menu today :

Marlin, flown in daily
Caviar, milked from the sturgeon
__same day__.
Baby elvers tempura
Foal with white truffles and beets

If you are feeling adventurous
however :—

Order in advance
Panda Steak tartare
Centenarian turtle
Love Birds (served as a pair)
.not caught

We feed greed with excess
Animals consume animals
A hideous gastronomic bordello

Could not have got enough
Drunk customers queue for
helicopters —
I've been __Sated__

Paris Loves My Oui Oui
A Fashion Story

CONTEXT

A character so insecure that she seeks the affirmation of brand identity.

PRINCIPLES AT PLAY

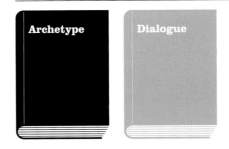

PARIS LOVES MY OUI OUI

How would I ever know? Ever know
how to? Where would I start?
This with that, under that over that.
It's unique and daring. Who says it is?
How do you know?
Your look says something to me. I read
it somewhere.
How could you ever pull that off?
I want to know how you know.
Where does it come from?

You're so confident mon bon vivant

I want to look in all the right places,
nooks and long forgotten crannies.
Places no one else has thought of, for
a while.
I want to rip out inspiration from the
best page
And stick it on my wall, let it form the
base of who I am today.
It will come round again. It's sure to.
I want to be the twist

You are original, the authentic article.
Great big puddles of delicious
newness that seem to drip from you.
I look at the reflection
It looks good on me
It's infectious
It will catch on
It must
Surely
Wildfire.

You're so confident mon bon vivant

I want the looks you get
Looks that say it all
You are directional
Going somewhere. Anywhere.
Who cares?

I want your look and the looks you get
I want them to stop and stare
And say how dare she mix and match
Her metaphor and influence.

How did she do that?
It looks as though she fell into that.
Without thought or common sense.
It will define the season, prompt the
masses to reconsider the mirror.
Let them. By the time they do, I will be
long gone.

I want to be photographed by a first
name only, a Klaus, an Arthur,
perhaps a Sam.
I want them all to pin me up and look
and point
And laugh at how little I seem to care
On the outside

I want to look like that
I want to look like you
I like what it says
I am your shadow
Your muse
Your acolyte

Brand Nation
A Story of Belief

Emotion beyond logic.

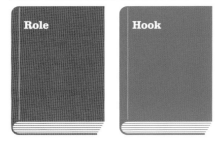

It feeds us, Inspires us, Defines us, sets us apart. It is all around us, everywhere, every second, It is within us, It sets our targets, creates our heroes, It is our heritage and our legacy. It drives us on.

There is always

POSSI

BLITY

WITH PRIDE

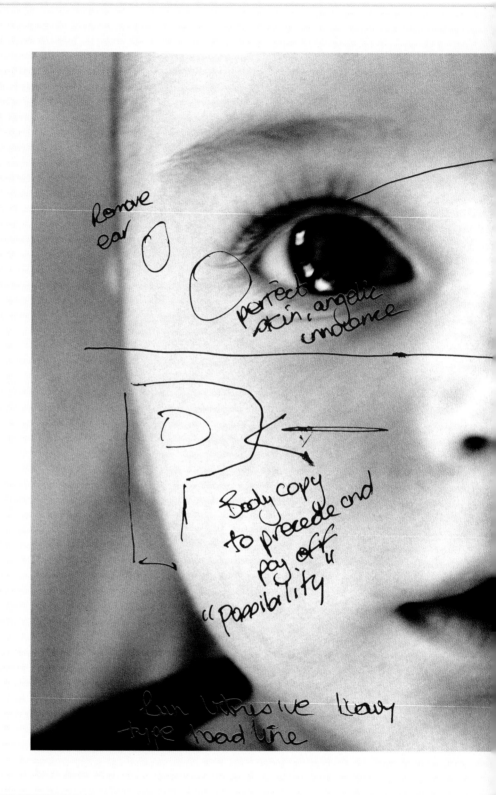

Ask Lubetkin

A few lines that hint at a world of action and intrigue. A poster for a film that doesn't exist lays bare the tools of the marketeer.

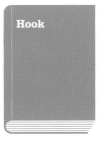

WHEN ALL ELSE FAILS...

ASK LUB

"HE HAS A SHORT FUSE AND IT'S A BIG BOMB"

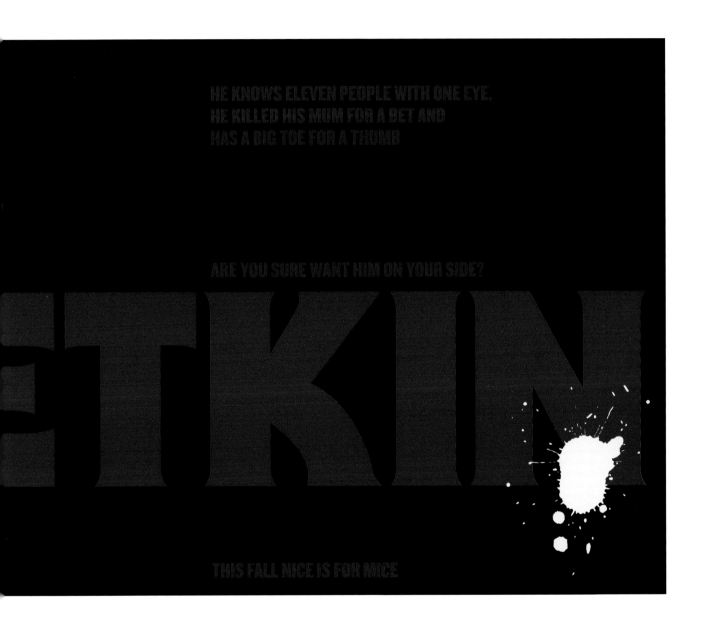

HE KNOWS ELEVEN PEOPLE WITH ONE EYE,
HE KILLED HIS MUM FOR A BET AND
HAS A BIG TOE FOR A THUMB

ARE YOU SURE WANT HIM ON YOUR SIDE?

THIS FALL NICE IS FOR MICE

I Hear You
A Healing Story

Make Believe was asked to work on a project that asked "Could advertising stop terrorism?" After listening to the people of the community where some of the 7/7 bombers lived, we thought the answer could be "yes".
This is the story that we created into a campaign idea.

PRINCIPLES AT PLAY

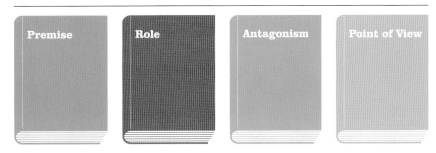

BOMB DISPOSAL EQUIPMENT

There are two sides to every story.
We want to listen.
We want to create an environment
that will help stop the need for terror.
Lend your ear to the debate.
Keep the discussion alive

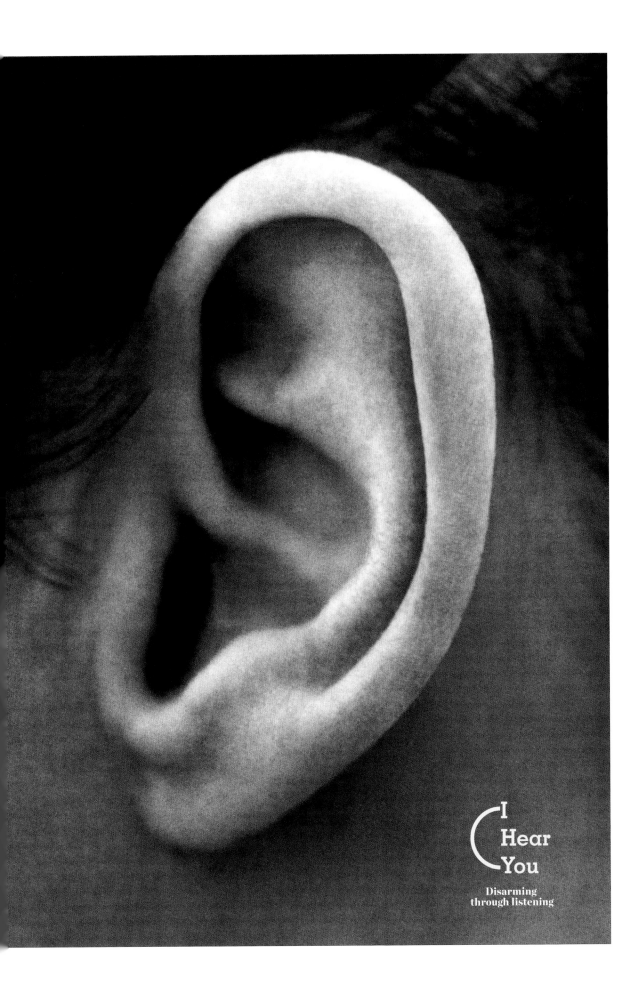

I
Hear
You

**Disarming
through listening**

What Can I Tell You?
An Ongoing Story

Giving this book a back story.

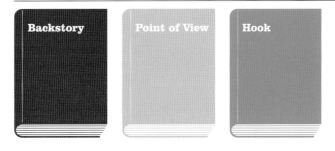

WHAT CAN I TELL YOU?

I am a storyteller in advertising. I am called a copywriter. I write stories that turn products into brands, commodities into stories. I give them meaning, character, colour. Enough so the consumer can make the emotional connection and see the need for this thing in their lives. There's no such thing as logic in storytelling - emotion sells.

I am a film director. I bring stories to life. I try to show characters in all their dimensions. I try to entice the viewer into my world, make them connect with the story – emotion connects us all.

I am a photographer. I take photos to tell stories and bring them to life. People project their own stories into my pictures.

I am a writer. I create worlds, make a point or two so people can enter for a while and make a connection.

Wherever I have turned in my life, professionally and personally, I have been faced with story. I didn't make that connection for a long time. We constantly tell stories, we use them to communicate, teach, influence, entertain and sell, it matters not what form they take, visual, written or otherwise, they are stories that follow the same principles. We are all storytellers.

All we have are stories. They prove our existence.
They are everywhere

I tell stories and I sell stories

66
A Story of Comings and Goings

A door provides a unique point of view to talk about the emotional roller coaster of life. Like a camera, a silent witness visually. A door could stand as an image for many things.

PRINCIPLES AT PLAY

66

This is a story

Of comings and goings
Ebb and flow
Arrivals, departures
Our flimsy barrier that defines our world.

Slammed behind me
Running away.

Of heroes' returns
Singing and laughing
Head to where I come from, home.

Of happy thresholds
A gateway to safety
Where eyes get weary
On the shortest journey in parents' arms.

Of news arriving, dropping
Friends popping in
Hauling happy shopping
Past the point of no return.

Of first footing, welcoming the new
Out with the old and unwanted.

The breath, the rhythm
The melodies of my life

Of beginnings, of journeys
So glad to be back with memory chock full
Of out there

Of familiar smells
Of next door yells and screams
This bustle, percussive sounds that reassure

Of this hideaway
Where I can lick a wound
Share a worry
Recharge
Heal.

This is mine.
My world
That I adore
Behind this simple door
Marked 66.

TRAN
CEN—
DEN

Come Here Today
A Story of Redemption

The shooting script for a short film starring Rhys Ifans and Rita Tushingham, which slowly reveals the moments of perfect clarity of a man in the moments before his death. Mixed settings add to the intrigue as the characters are revealed.

PRINCIPLES AT PLAY

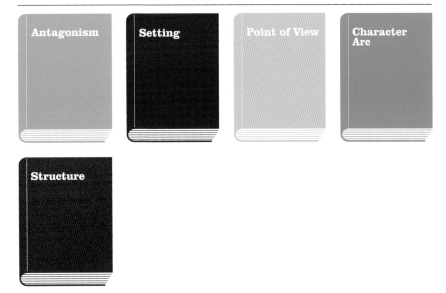

Antagonism · Setting · Point of View · Character Arc · Structure

COME HERE TODAY

VISION: BLACK & WHITE. ALL OF ALEX'S SCENES HAVE SOUND, ALL OTHER SCENES ARE, FOR THE MOST PART SILENT, EXCEPT WHERE NOTED.

INT. BEDROOM. DAY

We see a black suit, white shirt and tie hanging neatly on the back of a door. Behind the door we hear a man whistling and a shower running.

INT. FUNCTION ROOM. DAY

B&W & SILENT. In a large plain room, the afternoon sunlight streams through the drawn curtains wherever it can. The room is busy and smoky, a strange and soundless mixture of bright young things and a much older group. All are dressed formally and quite beautifully, even the ageing look timelessly glamorous. It is impossible to pinpoint what decade we are in. There is an intimacy accentuated by the silence.

Guests drink wine and industrial-sized spirits. They either pick or gorge themselves on a mountainous cold buffet at one end of the room. The scales of a salmon glint, lobsters rub shoulders with langoustines, exotic fruit are trapped inside quivering jellies. The scene is ripe for gluttony. Glasses are full, plates piled high.

We observe some of the players close up around the room. We notice details of slight decay behind the veneer of glamour: smudged mascara, smoke billowing from an open and perfectly made up mouth, a food stain on an expensive dress. A middle aged woman is clearly drunk and is in the process of embarrassing herself. She stubs out a lipstick-covered cigarette butt on a plate of untouched food.

CUT TO:

EXT. ROAD. DAY

Alex, 35, is now immaculately dressed in the suit and tie as he walks along, hands in pockets. He whistles as he walks. He is the only person around. Happiness bursts from him. He ruffles his squeaky clean hair for something to do with his restless hands. He constantly adjusts his tie and runs his finger inside the collar of his shirt.

V.O.

I know I've never seen it before. Not close, not even near. Like that game we played when we were kids, cold, freeeezing cold! A country bloody mile away.

CUT TO:

INT. FUNCTION ROOM. DAY

The guests have split into smaller groups. They smile politely. We're not sure what they're saying but you get the idea that the talk is small, even tiny. In CU, however, they look so glamorous, shiny and lustrous...such pretty things. They fiddle with their props, their drinks, cigarettes, the ice clinking in their glasses, the food on their plates. Details. Their mouths move, words are formed. In silence they are meaningless. The gloss is fading, decadence rearing its head in the smoky room. The buffet has been ransacked, pillaged.

V.O.

We overcomplicate, elaborate, always, putting things in the way, obstructions, hazards. Tripping ourselves up, avoiding the issue. Constant distractions. Pleasantries.

CUT TO:

EXT. ROAD. DAY

Alex stops. We pull back to reveal that, dressed to the nines, he's in the middle of nowhere. He takes off his tie, raises his collar and meticulously reties it. Happy, he moves off again.

V.O

I like the way I feel today. Lighter, a bit older (a beat) and clean. Squeaky clean. I feel like I've got hours to spare. A bit of space, room to breathe. It's a special day today. Growing up is a special thing.

CUT TO:

INT. FUNCTION ROOM. DAY

B&W SILENT. The leader of one particular group of guests, Vincent, a good looking young man, is dishevelled, drunk and pensive. He gulps from a pint, bolts a short and stares at nothing in particular. His girlfriend, a pretty young thing, tipsy herself, feigns concern and tries to slow him down.

She wears clothes altogether more revealing than anyone else and the camera lingers on her cleavage a little too long for our comfort. His friends look on. He pushes her away and lights up. He drops his drink on the floor. His girlfriend admonishes him whilst flirting with the group. Her lack of real care is transparent. "Look at me," she screams in silence. Vincent accepts another unnecessary drink. He's holding it together...just.

V.O.

There is never enough. Never will be. And there will always be some,

and they know who they are, for whom the agenda will always, firmly, unswervingly and unfailingly, be (a beat) themselves.

CUT TO:

EXT.CORRIDOR.SAME
A stunning girl, beautifully dressed, walks towards the door opening into the gathering when the heel breaks from one of her vertiginous heels. Gretchen stumbles.

CUT TO:

INT.FUNCTION ROOM.SAME
The whole room pauses as Gretchen walks into the room. She holds her shoes in her hands, her long dress now scraping the floor. She is barefoot. She turns every head as she crosses the room to the group we've seen previously and leaves a trail of whispering and judgement. The energy of a hundred eyes burns a hole in her back. She greets each of the group, leaving a special hug for drunken boy. A drink arrives for her.

V.O.
(wolf whistles)

CUT TO:

EXT.COUNTRYSIDE.DAY
Alex stands and looks at a never ending view. He is mesmerised by it.

V.O.
You can see for miles today.
You can see forever.

CUT TO:

INT.FUNCTION ROOM.DAY
Gretchen has the attention of all the boys but keeps her poise and her eye on Vincent. Vincent's girlfriend vies for attention.

V.O.
In the beginning I was just glad she'd have me, I worked tirelessly for her affection. I was overjoyed when she gave in, when her defences crumbled. Never thought I deserved her attention.

I thought she was just like me. (a long beat) How wrong I was. A tear drops from Gretchen's eye. Everything around her drops to blackness.

CUT TO:

INT.BAR.NIGHT
From the blackness we see that the tear has become a puddle of spilt drink on a table in a bar. Alex and Gretchen are the last in there. A waiter cleans tables and keeps an eye on a clearly drunken Alex.

The atmosphere is charged, the silence brooding, deafening. Alex drains an unnecessary glass of wine determined to finish the bottle. Gretchen simmers. She looks as though she could kill or cry with not much in between. We look into her face and we see she is struggling to comprehend Alex. In the silence that swamps us, this seems to go on for an uncomfortably long time.

Alex offers her a drink. This proves to be the detonator switch. Gretchen starts to scream. In the silence, this seems bizarre, disjointed. We struggle to understand the words on her lips.

Alex just sits there looking scared... and drunk. Suddenly, out of nowhere, we hear a couple of lines of dialogue explode out of the silence.

GRETCHEN
(crying uncontrollably)
Say something Alex, just say something! Anything, for God's sake, just try and help me understand why you do these things. Do you hate me?

She picks up his half full wine glass.

GRETCHEN (CONT'D)
Is this more important than me? Is this your true love my darling?

The silence returns as she carries on shouting. She smashes the glass under her hand.

V.O.
It never struck me that she would fall in love with me. I hadn't planned for that. This was all just a game that I thought I'd won, the moment she was mine. But there was complexity and depth. And me that was shallow as a puddle.(a beat) Splish splosh!

Gretchen stops her outburst as quickly as she began and is crying. Alex is frozen, emotionless. He reaches for the wine bottle and drinks from it. He has no idea what to do, how to give himself to her.

V.O. (CONT'D)
I'm a slow learner you see.

CUT TO:

EXT.COUNTRYSIDE.DAY
Alex stands at a stone water trough in a field, his jacket neatly folded beside him. He cups his hands and gathers the cool water to his face. The water is crystal clear as a fish swims. The water makes a gentle

sound as the fish breaks the surface.

V.O.

I need so little now, to fill me up.
We see a reflection of contentment.
To the top.

CUT TO:

INT. FUNCTION ROOM. DAY

CU. on an extravagant patisserie cake on the buffet table as a slice is cut out with a silver cake slice. Gretchen looks out of a window for inspiration. In the middle of the room, a beautiful older woman holds court. The matriarch. She is perfectly turned out, diamonds glimmer in her ears. She eats a large piece of the cake and then washes it down with champagne. Childlike. She chats with many men, young and old. She seems to hold them to her. They seem mesmerised. We sense dark within her. A man approaches her.

MAN

Beautiful, (a beat) just beautiful.

She takes it in her stride.
Of course she does.

MOTHER
(smiling)
Thank you so much.

C.U. The woman's mouth as she eats the cake. She can't get enough in her mouth. She pokes it in with dainty fingers.

V.O.

The consummate consumer.
The glamorous glutton.

CU. She talks with her mouth full. Her gestures are exaggerated. She is talking at someone.

V.O. (CONT'D)

Well, I had to get it from somewhere.

MOTHER

And I tell you (tapping her fingers on her plate), if they told me once they told me a thousand times, you will not find freesias anywhere at this time of the year. Won't I just?', I said (smiling knowingly)

C.U. on her mouth, cake crumbs. The diamonds in her ear. She carries on.

MOTHER (CONT'D)

They thought I was mad to bring in caterers from such a distance...but I don't see anyone complaining, in fact I don't see much of the buffet left. They are good, (she takes a sip of champagne) very, very good. You should have some.

We see her son, Vincent. It is he whom she addresses. He is drunk, he has been crying. He can make no sense of anything.

MOTHER (CONT'D)

People notice the details. It's all they remember. Don't ever forget that. It's what I use to say to both of you. God is in the details. Oh yes. Well, I've done my best and that's all you can ask, I suppose.

CU. on her face. She looks tired. The camera creeps towards her and leaves the crowd behind. Now we just see her face, sadness written on it despite best efforts.

V.O.

That veneer, a thin paint job. There's only so much pleasure that a bit of cake can give, so to speak.

CUT TO:

EXT. COUNTRYSIDE. DAY

Alex stands looking out across the valley. Content.

V.O.

When I was a kid, I used to go swimming on Fridays. In the winter, I'd run home in the freezing cold, get fish and chips on the way. I'd be on my own in the darkness of the living room, fire on, warming up, filling up, tired, safe. Everything in its place. I thought that was just about perfect. (a long beat) I'm there again.

He starts to walk again, stops, ties his laces, buffs his polished shoes and moves off with purpose.

CUT TO:

INT. FUNCTION ROOM. DAY

Gretchen walks towards Vincent who reels, drunk. She pushes his girlfriend out of the way. She's come to save him.

CUT TO:

EXT. A FIELD. DAY

Alex walks along a path in a field.

V.O.

I understand now. The sacrifice and the point of view. The cross words and the black moods. The distance, the difference, the lack of understanding. The duty and diligence and the desire to improve and guide.

Alex has started to jog. The smile on his face is somehow wider than ever. The field climbs quickly into the evening horizon. He relishes the effort.

V.O. (CONT'D)
I understand the frustration. I know you were there really, just tuned in on a different wavelength, and getting static.

CUT TO:

INT.FUNCTION ROOM.DAY
Gretchen takes the drink out of Vincent's hand. She leads him away from the herd and across the room towards the door. They all look at her. She has taken control. She walks past the mother, who acknowledges her. She knows that Gretchen has the measure of her.

CUT TO:

EXT.HILLTOP.DAY
Alex reaches the top of the hill. He gets his bearings and sees his destination. He is euphoric and he sets off on the final bit of his journey.

V.O.
I know now how being normal must have seemed so strange. How it put you on the outside looking in.

CUT TO:

EXT.FUNCTION ROOM.DAY
Gretchen has led Vincent outside. The mother follows at a distance to see where she's taking her youngest. The brother stops, grabs Gretchen and tries to kiss her. She pushes him away. She looks at the mother who averts her gaze nonchalantly. She looks at Vincent for an eternity, puzzled. Gretchen throws her

shoes in a bin and leaves. The mother regains her composure, leaves Vincent and goes back into the party. Vincent is alone.

CUT TO:

EXT.COUNTRYSIDE.DAY
There is someone in the distance walking towards Alex. He is about 65 years old. He is distinguished, elegant and his face lights up when he sees his son. He too wears a black suit and tie with a white shirt. He waves. Alex waves back and they move ever closer together.

V.O.
There's no need now. I know. I know it all.

Alex runs the last few yards. He stops short of his father who looks him up and down, shaking his head. He holds his son's face, whose eyes now brim with tears. He pulls him in and almost crushes him with the ferocity of the love he has for him. They both cry. Reunited. In the middle of nowhere.

V.O. (CONT'D)
There is no need for words any more. They just get in the way.

They just smile at each other, the son locked in his father's arms. We can lip read as Alex tells his father.

ALEX
I love you dad.

His father takes it in and we read his lips as he replies.

FATHER
I love you too, son.

His father hugs his son for all he's worth, like he will never let him go again and will protect him forever. He cries. Relief, happiness, sadness. Together.

CUT TO:

INT.A BEDROOM.NIGHT
Alex lies dying. We know not why. He is lit by a single shaft of light like an angel. In C.U. His face is covered in sweat but his smile is serene. He is cradled in his father's arms who comforts him. He is in his death throes but he is at peace.

His father strokes his head and reassures him with that smiling face. Alex passes away and his body goes limp. His father continues to hold him.

CUT TO:

EXT.FUNCTION ROOM.DAY
Gretchen stands by herself. Angry. Demonstrative. Grief stricken. Genuine.

CUT TO:

INT.BEDROOM.NIGHT
The bedroom door swings open and Gretchen and Vincent find Alex's body. Gretchen scrambles to him, distraught. We watch the aftermath as they struggle to understand the implications. She is beside herself. Gretchen lies on Alex's limp body. Vincent stands by the door, confused, unable to process the event.

CUT TO:

EXT.COUNTRYSIDE.DAY
Alex and his father walk away, arm in arm, in conversation. Animated. Friends. Reunited.

TITLES ROLL

I'm Under a Bus I am
Some Final Thoughts

This story uses first person speech to investigate a touchy subject from an everyday angle. The ultimate premise made more comfortable by avoiding anything too profound.

I'M UNDER A BUS I AM

So this is it. Today is the day.

It seems so utterly random.

I can't move my head to look. It really doesn't hurt. I feel warm.

I can see people running around. They are looking, but it's panic I see on their faces. They seem annoyed that curiosity got the better of them.

A bus! How the fuck can you fail to see a bus? I've made some mistakes, but not seeing a bus and paying for it with your life is a tough one.

I don't feel any different. I can't see a white light or anyone waiting, none of that shit. But I think I'm dying. I feel like I'm being drained.

We got married on a Monday in December. Untraditional, you could say. It was the last thing Dad came to. He insisted on paying for the wedding and never flinched whenever Mum or I added something to the list. I think he'd prepared for that for a while.

He made a speech. He'd never made one before and I think I was a bit worried that he'd make a fool of me in front of everyone. It was an amazing speech. He told stories of my family that I'd never heard and he told them so eloquently. He had no notes and, once he started, no nerves. People laughed so hard. He made a real connection. Mum watched it a lot after he died and it comforted her. He knew she'd do that, didn't he?

I can hear quite a lot of distant noise. They look more alarmed now. I think they want to look like they are doing something until the professionals arrive. Stabilise me, but they don't know how. I'm beyond stabilising. Stop trying to fucking stabilise me.

Mum will have to bury me, her only daughter. I never wanted that. I've got so much to tell her now, but it's not possible.

I can imagine the policewoman calling at the house to see Eric to tell him I won't be coming home today. Ever. That is shocking.

I hope they all remember me.

Eric first took my Mum to the football five years ago. He took her as a bet.

I said that he would never do it. He did. She loved it. Now they both have season tickets. Most home games, off they go and click into some different world where my Mum talks statistics and apparently swears like a trooper. I've never heard her swear.

My kids? Eric will look after the kids. Who will cook for them? What will they eat? Who will know their favourite things?

All my stuff will remind everyone of me. They have lots of photos, lots of memories. They knew me, I think. Yes, they knew me.

Eric used to say it was about being rather than just doing. I loved that phrase. I think I've been.

Where is the stupid fucking ambulance? I pay my taxes and it's the only one I've ever needed. There will be an article in the local paper saying how disgraceful it is that the ambulance took so long to turn up. Could have saved my life. Little good that article will do me.

Before Ivy was born, we were greedy and wanted it all. We wanted a bigger house with a bigger garden. We wanted to go on better holidays. We constantly wanted. But wanting just carries on and the hole never really gets filled in. Then Ivy came and we woke up. The hole was full after that, life was happy.

An old woman is stroking my hair. That's nice. She's really calm. I think she knows I'm done for. She's kneeling on the road. She'll get ladders in her tights if she's not careful. She's lovely and she smells warm. She's a good woman. I can tell.

The curious keep peeking over her shoulder. I want to get up and kick them.

Blue lights. I can see the reflections in the puddles.

Things aren't that bad.

I hope my stories carry on. I hope they get better.

It's alright. I'm smiling.

De Kooning's shoes
An Inspirational Story

CONTEXT

I visited Willem De Kooning's studio in Long Island NY last year, where everything has been left exactly as it was the day that he passed away. An inspirational experience as you attempt to put all the pieces of the puzzle together, having previously only been aware of the end result of his labour. This photo that I took that day has always stood out as a story in itself.

PRINCIPLES AT PLAY

DE KOONING'S SHOES

STOR
IS OU
BUSI

Y
R
NESS

THE ALLURE OF STORY
by Paul Wilson

Our voracious appetite for stories means they are as conveniently available as food and drink in daily life. More than ever, we are awash with shape-shifting stories that spread like virus through every area of life. The art is deployed by a diverse range of storytellers, who may create empathy or educate, influence or persuade. Obvious sources are news, entertainment and education. Less obvious ones are politics, health and brand marketing. Doctors use stories to heal, coaches use stories to motivate, leaders use stories to inspire, companies use stories to sell, teachers use stories to enlighten, parents use stories to comfort.

The implications of such an explosion in storytelling's volume, intensity and consumption are immense and not yet entirely predictable. One effect we already see around us is the relentless search for new ways to engage audiences in content and delivery but there is more to come. We have seen many innovations in recent years, but they will be dwarfed by those we will see in the coming decade, when there will be a turning point in the art of storytelling with far greater implications than those that followed the invention of the printed book, television and cinema.

An analogy that may help to explain storytelling's growing influence is that of a long-living tree. The tree's trunk is the ancient art, which includes immeasurable incarnations of oral and written tradition. With every passing day it grows, drawing energy from the environment for its own lifeblood and that of its branches. The oldest branches, such as fables, fairy tales and poetry, are well established and continue to extend their reach, but most fascinating for storytellers is the exponential new growth of younger shoots and branches bearing richly exuberant foliage.

Visionary Stories

Influencing perception and meaning is familiar territory for story. For thousands of years it has been used, in oral, written and visual form, to pass down wisdom, to guide the next generation or influence opinion across gender, age, race and class.

Stories bless information with meaning, simplify complex issues, provide roles to play, honour the past, celebrate the present and create enticing futures in compelling fashion.

Storytelling, as influencing perception, may evoke the idea of fabricated or deceitful stories. But some of the greatest storytelling shares a more compelling vision of the truth that helps people believe. Just one high profile example of recent times is Al Gore's groundbreaking film *An Inconvenient Truth*, which acted as an 'inciting incident' to engage hundreds of millions in the environmental debate. Where politics failed to shift mass opinion, Hollywood may yet succeed. Britain's 2012 Olympic pitch illustrates another aspect of vision at work. By using a big budget film to tell a story of how the Games would inspire the next generation of athletes, the premise of the games and what was at stake in the decision making process changed.

None of this is new. Across the millennia and many cultures, story has been regularly deployed by governments, religions and outsiders who wish to change the system. Aristotle studied the power of story in Ancient Greece. Jesus was a prolific storyteller, Muhammad recounted his revelations. Ghandi used it to unite millions of Indians in their quest for independence. Mandela's life story has inspired millions. The principles remain the same, but the media, and hence the scale and speed, of story's distribution has dramatically changed. Barack Obama's understanding of story's power to engage, influence

40,000BC
Aboriginal songline

3000BC
Gilgamesh
clay tablets Sumerian cuneiform
collective

3,150BC
Tomb of Seti I, Abydos temple
stone
hieroglyphs, paintings, sculptures
Egyptian
collective

1,200-200BC
Tanakh (Old Testament)
manuscript
prose
Hebrew
collective

776BC
Olympic Games
performance
body exercises, sports, speech
Greek
collective

551-479BC
The Analects
oral teaching, manuscript
speech and prose
Chinese
K'ung-tse (Confucius)

500-300BC
Rāmāyana
recitals and manuscript
verse
Hindi
collective

628
letters
Muhammad
collective

868
Buddhist Diamond Sutra
printed book
collective

1350
Hagoromo
performance
dialogue, poetry, music, dance, costume
Japanese
Noh theatre

1455
Gutenberg Bible
printed book
verse
Latin
Johannes Gutenberg

1508-1512
Sistine Chapel ceiling, Creation and Last Judgement
pigments on plaster
fresco painting
Michaelangelo

and motivate people towards change, and the use he made of it during his 2008 election campaign will surely go down in history. Part of that is his quest for a new vision of the USA. Another is the way he used a new storytelling template that befits our digital age to give people a starring role in bringing about change. As a result he has breathed new life into the 'American dream'.

We believe the call for story today should not be underestimated. To some that may be a heady thought, yet great storytellers have a track record of changing the world we live in. World leaders, industries, organisations and brands know good storytelling can be the difference between success and failure.

Who can afford to look away from its power?

Digital storytelling

The internet is the new digital campfire inspiring a proliferation in storytelling. Free, flexible, real time unlimited digital space is creating a new generation of storytellers ready to challenge accepted practice. The traditional three-act structure of beginning, middle and end has already evolved many times, but this is an area of storytelling we believe will be transformed by the audience playing new roles as they engage with open, free flowing structures.

Reality shows, computer games and online forums represent a storytelling arc that often goes unrecognized. The new formats engage us so compellingly because they play by new rules. They thrive across multiple platforms, have multiple beginnings and endings as well as different levels of immersion and experience. By going 'live', inviting the audience to play a role in plot development in the here and now, some stories will become unrecognisable, in both presentation and execution, from the oral tradition from which they began. Established storytellers face growing competition from new ones deploying the same principles in new forms.

Probably the clearest example lies in the modern gaming industry. Today it shares more similarities with Hollywood than with its own past. Online games now come with comprehensive back stories, sophisticated casting and visionary settings, attracting tens of millions of people into their story world on a daily basis and encouraging them to play a role, direct the story and, in turn, evolve its art.

At the same time established storytellers working in theatre, publishing and new digital media have honed their skills at entertaining audiences with startling effect. Familiar formats such as television soap operas, cinema trilogies, talent shows, pantomime and autobiography are constantly pushing 'tried and trusted' approaches for hooking us in. A good example of this are the burgeoning television talent shows, such as *Pop Idol* and *X Factor*, which top the viewings ratings the world over. Only a few years ago such shows would simply provide a stage for contestants to compete on talent, but all that has changed. Nowadays, we are presented with three dimensional characters complete with hopes, dreams, fears and failures. Their journey is told from multiple points of view and includes inner and outer conflicts and numerous turning points designed to heighten engagement.

Sophisticated characterisation is likely to continue for a long time as it trades off our unconscious attraction to archetypes. We already have robots as lead characters, cartoon fish with inner conflicts and a host of nursery rhyme characters with complex psychological make ups. We find characterisation so addictive because understanding characters better is a door to understanding ourselves better. A side effect of this fascination with character interrogation is the growing obsession with celebrity in society and the intimate levels of detail we demand of stories about them.

Another principle in which the entertainment industry leads is the development of genre to reflect societal norms and values. Primary genres such as 'love story' have evolved from relatively straightforward romantic quests through to multi-plot structures that challenge values around sexuality, loyalty and faith. Even modern genres such as the 'psychological thriller' have evolved dramatically over the past few decades. Here antagonism has moved from the external world to the internal world. Nowadays, we are not only aware of the threat from

1596
Romeo and Juliet
performance and
printed book
verse English
William Shakespeare

1605
Relation aller Fürnemmen und gedenckwürdigen Historien
earliest printed newspaper
Strasbourg
Johann Carolus

1697
Contes de Temps Passé (Tales of Past Times)
oral tradition and printed book
fairy stories
French
Charles Perrault

1719
Robinson Crusoe
printed book
novel
English
Daniel Defoe

1792
A Vindication of the Rights of Woman
printed book
manifesto
English
Mary Wollstonecraft

1859
On The Origin of Species
printed book and
public debate
prose and speech
English
Charles Darwin

1887
Animal Locomotion
printed book
stop-motion photography
English
Eadweard Muybridge

1893
Skrik (The Scream)
oil, tempera, pastel on cardboard
portrait painting
Edvard Munch

1905
Photoelectric Effect, Brownian Motion, Special Relativity Matter and Energy Equivalence
four scientific papers proving the theory of relativity
equations, calculations, prose
Annalen der Physik
German Physics Journal
Albert Einstein

1922
Ulysses
printed book
prose
Irish English
James Joyce

strangers, but also the 'shadow' lurking inside ourselves, a reflection of the growing interest and understanding of psychology in many Western societies. Could the next evolution reflect a growing trend for us to be more connected with other cultures? This is already happening in areas such as modern opera with for example, *Monkey Journey to the West*, which creatively blends Eastern and Western music, dance and performance art and was a joint conception of the creative team behind the virtual band Gorillaz and actor and director Chen Shi-zheng.

Putting Story to Work

Insight into the evolution of storytelling and its principles in entertainment and the wider world is far from academic. Storytelling is based upon known principles and as such is a learnt skill which promises a way of engaging large numbers of people on multiple levels in an increasingly noisy and cluttered world. This has not been lost on some of the worlds most powerful organisations, which are deploying the art with pace.

Most of us are familiar with business storytelling from advertising culture. Classic examples known across five continents include the enigmatic 'Marlborough cowboy', which uses archetype and setting to sell cigarettes. Budweiser's 'Wassup' campaign uses contagious new dialogue to promote and sell alcohol. Louis Vuitton sells luxury travel items by reminding us that every journey is a story with a rolling cast of famous celebrities.

From that framework companies have sometimes moved on to see themselves as stories which guide strategy and communications. Disney 'is' a story of magic, Harley Davidson a story of freedom, Nike a story of competition. By placing story at the heart of organisational and brand thinking, companies have become more effective at creating consistent and compelling worlds. Apple computers, in our own time, for example, have created a stylish conceptual world of information technology that we can inhabit and enjoy. Traditional brand promotion has relied heavily upon 'one way' communication, but this is now being

challenged by more interactive options. The advertising industry is using the principle of role to find new ways for the audience to experience stories and, in turn, engage with them at a deeper level. We may see this online with story formats that encourage the audience to introduce new characters, to change story direction and redesign aspects of story world. Storytelling to sell is becoming more open, playful and coauthored.

It is also increasingly giving us – or you – new profiles in the story. Dove skincare challenges tradition in the beauty sector by using customers, not models, in its campaigns to promote its products. Agent Provocateur, the London based lingerie company, gives the customer the starring role as secret seductress. IKEA products are sold incomplete and require you to finish them off. That is not only a question of cutting costs - it's also part of the trend for manufacturers and advertisers to give us a starring role.

New Branches: Healing, Not-for-Profit, Teaching

It's also an incredibly exciting time for storytellers who are stretching our understanding of human experience into diverse new areas of life.

Healthcare has always used storytelling to help people engage with their condition. Most practitioners have personal 'bedside' stories that help patients to understand what is happening to them and deal with their situation. That is developing further today. *Cancer Vixen* is a best selling graphic novel that takes this to another level by switching genre and point of view, and dramatising character dilemmas. Written by a survivor of breast cancer, it brings to the real life story of what it is like to be diagnosed and treated and to beat the disease a power no medical document could ever have. This masterful piece of storytelling allows the reader to experience the emotional rollercoaster, intellectual conundrums and social pressures that come with diagnosis and has led a rush of other health-based graphic novels.

My Cancer Year and *Black Dog* – the latter dealing with depression - both use storytelling to engage

1927
The Jazz Singer
film
dialogue, music, dance, song, costume
American English
collective

1928
Plane Crazy
(Mickey Mouse's first appearance)
film
animated cartoon, recorded soundtrack
American English
Walt Disney company

1935
Ariel: A Shelley Romance
First title published
paperback book
fiction
English
Penguin Books
André Maurois

1936
Guernica
paint and canvas
abstract art
Pablo Picasso

1938
War of the Worlds
radio
fiction narrated as news item
English
H.G. Wells and Orson Welles

1940
The Dictator
satirical film
black and white film, soundtrack
American English
Charles Chaplin

1953
Coronation of Queen Elizabeth II
TV broadcast to 20 million viewers in the UK and 500 million worldwide
script and improvised speech
English and other languages

1958
West Side Story
stage musical and film
musical score, script, choreography
American English
Leonard Bernstein, Jerome Robbins

1950s-60s
The Times They Are a Changin'
vinyl record
folk song
American English
Bob Dylan

patients at an appropriate level for healing. Principles such as role, dialogue and inciting incident help patients engage with, and better manage, their conditions. They find tactical uses in public health campaigns, community support and seasonal inoculations, but some of the greatest advances are associated with new treatments for psychological conditions that use personal storytelling to manage individual narratives, values and identity.

Numerous other branches of storytelling have emerged in different contexts: drama therapy, spiritual development, social cohesion, drug rehabilitation, crime analysis, tourism, online retail and real estate. In many of these functional contexts stories are used as 'dress rehearsals for life', allowing us to try on new perspectives, truths and experiences as comfortably and pleasurably as trying on clothing. For this reason alone, storytelling is an increasingly valuable tool for modern life.

Let us look at just one of these areas in more detail. Storytelling is increasingly being used in not-for-profit sectors. Charities, museums, religions and lobby groups are all using stories to fuel their growth and influence. Some, such as Oxfam and Greenpeace, have a long standing storytelling tradition that has always shared stories from the front line to engage us. A different approach is being used in Ireland with the 'Food Dudes' campaign to encourage healthy eating. This uses food-inspired super hero characters to engage children in diet and nutrition in a way that is hard for formal education to take on. One wonders how more compelling points of view, dialogue and dramatisations will help such causes in the future. How long before we experience voices directly and provide assistance in real time so that we directly change the course of life or community stories in front of our very eyes?

Education is yet another area of life set to be revolutionised by advances in the art. Most of the world's greatest thinkers from Aristotle to Einstein have used imaginary worlds to solve problems and today still, despite the fact-based emphasis of western teaching, most teachers deploy storytelling principles to some degree. Switching point of view is important, for

example to the subatomic level in physics. Art students study the narrative of paintings to deepen their appreciation. History studies now allow a more personal experience of immersion in the past and in the future will allow us to move freely around virtual story worlds, touching and feeling certain aspects so they become ever more real. We may be able to change character, point of view, scenes and endings at the press of a button, thus transforming not only the entertainment value of such experiences but also their educational value.

The end is a new beginning

With such a formidable and emotive subject as story it is inevitable that any projections of the future will result in heated discussions. We hope. The proliferation of storytelling's branches and foliage today invites us to do that together. For us that is the heart of the matter.

One final point: the end but also the beginning of story. Whether old or new, great stories engage us intellectually, emotionally and spiritually, sometimes all at the same time. The courtship may happen over years or in some cases within a heartbeat, without you being fully aware of it, for stories talk to archetypal needs deep within our subconscious minds and influence our perception, behaviour and sense of self. Love, beauty, passion, fear and other aspects of what makes us human exist beyond logic. As such, they must be reached by other means. Stories do that. They may fuel desire, crush beliefs, question personal truths, expose fears and reveal weaknesses.

In this most delicate of seductions, a great story also requires us to play a part. Fantasy castles, the brave hero, war-torn lands, crushing defeat, romantic encounters and broken hearts are classic story elements, but so, too, is our personal interpretation. Our judgement is drawn in to evaluate characters, our point of view to solve a mystery. Great storytellers draw you into a web, then manage engagement by the second until a dramatic shift occurs. We experience the story first hand, anticipate turns and emotionally feel for characters. Unawares we become the real stars of the show. The story becomes our story. Remember the greatest story is the one you've never told.

• • •

1963
'I Have a Dream'
live and broadcast speech sermon
scripted and improvised
American English
Martin Luther King

1967
Sergeant Pepper's Lonely Hearts Club Band
vinyl LP record
English
The Beatles (music, lyrics),
Peter Blake (collage, artwork)

1971
I'd Like to Buy the World a Coke
radio, television, cinema, music, posters
song and slogan
American English
Coca Cola

1982
Just Say No
global anti drugs campaign
tv,posters,radio
American English
phrase originally coined by Nancy Reagan

1995
Toy Story
film
Pixar technology computer animation and soundtrack
American English and dubbed into many languages

1997
JK Rowling publishes the first book in the *Harry Potter* series
one of the most successful of all time
book, film, computer games
translated into 77 languages.

2001
9/11 plane attacks
video and TV
documentary footage
with soundtrack
languages worldwide

2003
Second Life
virtual 3D electronic technology
dialogue script, digital computer animation
English and other languages
individual computer users.

2008
US presidential campaign (Democrat, Barack Obama)
live speech and multimedia (music, internet, mobile phone, TV, video)
American English
collective

THREE VIEWS OF STORY
Edward Booth-Clibborn, Simon Aboud and Paul Wilson

EDWARD BOOTH-CLIBBORN: Do you regard the craft of story as a tool?

SIMON ABOUD: More precisely, we see the principles of story as a toolkit. We believe many people in advertising and marketing tell stories intuitively, but don't sit down to think about how story works. We are saying, if you know the principles you are going to be a lot better equipped and you'll have a new set of skills.

PAUL WILSON: In our industry, it's surprising, isn't it, how many big companies tell stories by intuition? Disney was a story of magic right from the beginning. Harley Davidson started out as a story of freedom and it still is that. But we're saying, you need to go beyond intuition because everything is sharpened. We're competing in a busier world - it's more cluttered and noisy, there's more competition for our attention in every sector. Story principles can help cut through that, whatever the challenge.

EBC: Well advertising also uses story. In the early days advertising was just product information, but in the 1950s the Americans changed that. They came up with one-liners. Often genius one-liners. Those are stories, used to get people to identify and engage with the product. The breakthrough in Britain came when we started using our own colloquial language.

SA: Yes, advertising uses the same principles as a fairy tale to make a connection.

EBC: Fairy tales are a significant example. They have a certain universal wisdom that crosses cultural boundaries and resonates with us all. A great commercial can be like a fairy tale in that respect.

SA: Yes, but we go further. We're suggesting applying storytelling principles to wider thinking so you take storytelling into the heart of an organization and use it to articulate whatever you need to communicate through any media - online, tv, cinema, print, new products. We're saying story is the foundation of all communication.

EBC: Is that entirely new? When Marshall McLuhan wrote about the medium as the message in the 1960s, his main interest was to communicate a story visually and verbally in the simplest possible terms.

PW: Well, visual media are certainly dominant and growing. Storytelling in the global village doesn't need verbal language. The keys are character archetypes and story arcs which communicate universally. But we think more in terms of formats than media. We are trying to get people to appreciate just how many formats stories work in. Once you understand the product on the shelf is telling you a story, the guy on TV is telling you a story, the bus is telling you a story, your friends are telling you a story, then you begin to appreciate its power. Stories are shape-shifters. You can have one story in twenty formats. For example, is a Caravaggio painting a story?

EBC: Yes of course. A great painting tells a story, your eye looks at it and goes around and gets information. The eye must stay in the picture. A visual story has got to work as a unit and keep your attention. That's very important. It may be old fashioned, but it works. I believe the visual element needs principles like those of any storyteller weaving a story to enthrall the listener or reader, but I wouldn't have twenty, just three. Pitch, pace and pause.

SA: That's because you have raised it to an intuitive level. I think if you analysed those three ideas, you'd find more principles at play.

EBC: You can find as many as you want, but a spark of creativity, inspiration, call it what you will, though is instinctive.

So, going back to what you are about, are there any limits to story formats?

SA: We believe story is everywhere. In a business context, marketing or whatever, that means, very simply, communicating is no longer about only TV or cinema or press or radio or internet. Paul was talking about engagement in shops – that is one of hundreds of new forms of engagement that are all around us. We're suggesting that any form of engagement will be more effective if it is about storytelling. We'd say there should be no difference between our engagement with a great film, story or brand.

PW: As soon as you engage an audience, whether it's emotional or just functional, you're half way there. We focus on how to take that to the next level - how to help people deliver engagement effectively.

EBC: What do you do when clients come to you?

PW: In essence we help clients 'tell and sell' the most compelling versions of their story. There are two distinct levels, organisational storytelling, which brings together vision and strategy, and brand storytelling, which is strategy plus communications.

EBC: Could you break those down in more detail?

PW: Organisational storytelling includes helping clients share their future story, giving stakeholders a role to play and giving strategy an emotional charge. People don't remember strategies but great stories are unforgettable because we are meaning-machines, we need stories to make sense of the world. I'm not sure how many people understand that.

EBC: What about the brand storytelling?

PW: A very important result of the clients seizing back the responsibility for engagement and control of their stories is, almost always, more consistent and compelling storytelling across brand activity. We help with management of every element from logos through to pack copy so it is consistent with the brand story we're trying to tell. Great brands don't have inconsistencies or contradictions anywhere in their story, from big budget advertisting through to in-store promotions. By story-authoring from the centre this becomes a possibility.

EBC: Who authors the stories?

SA: Our role is to help the clients themselves author the most powerful story for their brand and articulate it. Once they have the right story, it becomes much clearer how we are going to tell the story. In fact it becomes much clearer where we are going to tell it too. Also, if a client has a story that they have helped author and believe in then it is much, much easier to involve them in the creative process. From there we move on to identity and logo.

EBC: Isn't that what advertising agencies do?

SA: No. They create great stories around 'product' truths for specific advertising campaigns. We put story at the heart of the brand from day one and then let that organically inform advertising as well as every other aspect of a business.

EBC: With so many new channels available for storytelling, where is all this heading?

SA: I was discussing this with a client and put it to him that everyone is still playing by the rules of a very outdated marketing model. He agreed. If a client creates a story that is understood internally by everyone in the organisation then it should permeate all aspects of the business quite naturally. It will shape how they create new products and services and even how they hire staff. The creation of a strong central story unifies and simplifies. Looking at it that way, it doesn't matter how many channels are out there, they are simply outlets for the story.

PW: I'd differ slightly. I think the plethora of media opportunities requires greater clarity and consistency. When you're managing an international brand across markets it's very common to see multiple versions of the story in play. This can undermine brand equity and result in millions of dollars of ineffective communication. The secret is to face the future with a sound understanding of the story you are telling and share this with all those responsible for telling it. That way the story is interpreted consistently right across the board.

EBC: Give me some examples of stories you've created for clients.

PW: We've helped clients tell adventure stories, mystery stories, character driven stories and even love stories. A good organisational example is a project with the BBC to help define their story for the next ten years. We flipped the story to the audience's point of view and celebrated the wonderful symbiotic relationship the BBC enjoys with the British public because, at its heart, there's a story of mutual inspiration between audience and creative community. We helped Grolsch create an appropriate voice for the brand that reflects their uniquely 'Dutch' perspective on the world. Their story is enshrined in the line 'Untraditional since 1615' and brought to life in dialogue and exposition across packaging, promotions and advertising. This activity was rolled out in the UK as part of the 'Green Light District' promotional campaign that was a light hearted play on the infamous 'Red Light Districts' in Holland and their inventive use of language.

We have just finished designing a brand new logo and identity for the National Farmers Union which very accurately reflects their new story of growth and progress but without the story being in place it would have been an almost impossible sell

EBC: You work all around the world. So do you find differences in the role of storytelling in different cultures and, therefore, have to work in different ways?

PW: All cultures have their own traditions of storytelling that must be acknowledged and honored. But we are yet to find a place where the principles we work with do not apply, only twists and adaptations. We are currently working with Unilever on an international campaign that spans markets as diverse as South Africa, Dubai and India. In situations like this it is critical to author the fundamentals of the story such as premise, plot and lead character etc. from the centre so there is consistency. However, we then work in the regions to ensure the fundamentals apply as well as on how principles such as setting, exposition and dialogue can be used to make the story relevant and compelling for the local audience.

EBC: Where do you see the future of storytelling, especially in the virtual world? We cannot underestimate the influence of electronic media.

PW: It's a cliché isn't it, that advertising has gone from monologue to dialogue. If you stand back, it is clear the internet has blown that to another level. Whatever story you are telling, it's actually co-authored. You are not in charge of the story. You send the story out, people turn it round, make their interpretation of it and send it on through the world.

EBC: Wasn't that always the case with films, novels or even fairy stories?

PW: Yes, but we didn't send on co-authored stories in the same way. I think we'll also reach the point where we have experiences, for example in virtual storytelling, as 'realistic' as real world experiences. That means we will come to a defining moment in deciding storytelling's role in all our lives. I haven't got a down on that. It's just a natural evolution. Reality will win, but it will be an interesting blur, especially when you make it easy for people to experience life in a different character's shoes, because it may become so compelling and so exciting that it will blur whether they want to stay in the fictional character or go back to the real world. I tell myself stories all the time, that I'm a good dad, that I support Chelsea, but if that gets blurred with fictional characters I'm playing, that's interesting.

EBC: Well, there's a moral dilemma there, isn't there?

SA: Some people argue that brands are taking on the mantle of religion. Whether or not that is true, they have responsibilities. Brands have already allowed people to live through fictitious characters and to seek affirmation through the stories they tell.

PW: What's frightening, though, is that I am not sure people are aware they are doing it. That takes us into a whole new area – a quite different, but very good reason for showing how storytelling works, so people cannot be controlled by it.

EBC: How much do you see your work going into the realm of politics etc.? You work already with public services such as the BBC and the British government.

PW: An increasing amount of our time is spent working in the area of social change in which politics plays a major role. We've helped the British Government create a story set five years in the future to explain how it will improve border control against the threat of terrorism. We've helped Breakthrough Breast Cancer create High Street promotions and other mechanics to drive charitable giving. We've also helped non-profit political organizations such as Independent Diplomat get their story out into the world and raise awareness of countries and people that have a desperate need for diplomatic help but no means or skill to deliver it. Our work in such diverse areas of social change reinforces our belief that storytelling may be proactively used as a powerful force for good in the world.

EBC: Can you provide some examples of the techniques you use to engage clients in the challenge and opportunity for storytelling.

PW: Many of the techniques we use are adapted from the storytellers toolkit such as plotting engagement, character analysis and the dreaded art of re-writing! However, there are some techniques that we use to dramatically reveal the power of story to clients. When we start working with a client it is sometimes neccesary to demonstrate that there are many sides to every story. We do this by asking the core team to write down the story in their own words in silence and then share with the rest of the group. What follows are different interpretations of their own story usually with some pretty colourful variations! Then we ask them if they would like to hear the real version of their story before revealing a video of 'voxpops' that we have pre-recorded of their customers answering the same question. The exercise takes no more than an hour but is usually a pivotal moment as clients experience inconsistencies and conflicts first hand and realize they need to author a more consistent and compelling story from the centre.

Another good example is a technique called 'In their eyes' that we use to help clients see the world from their customers' point of view. Here we give each person a target audience profile (like a character sheet) and ask them to get into character whilst we interview them. What comes out of their mouths is a stream of beliefs and assumptions they are holding about their customer. This is an immersive insight experience with a punch as when the interview is finished we ask them to sit at the side as we bring into the room the actual people they have just role played and ask them the same set of questions. This is a great storytelling exercise as it requires people to change role and point of view then contrast their assumptions against reality.

SA: Another live issue for the future is the written versus the visual. Some people say the written word is dead.

EBC: I think since we live in a visual society, people are using visual things to tell a story, but the words haven't gone away.

SA: No. We anchor meaning with words. That happens in advertising too. The best ads we remember are the ones that require least time to get the back story.

EBC: But is that storytelling?

SA: In a sense, yes. It's reductive story telling. What I mean by that is, give me the whole book and I'll sum it up and engage you in a few words.

EBC: How would you sum it up?

SA: We are made of stories.

EBC: Great, that's the genius of advertising, but I'm still not sure if it's storytelling.

SA: Well, maybe more the science? Advertising is a business, part of the culture and maybe now it's in the very early days of becoming more of a science.

WHY WE CAN TELL YOU

Simon Aboud
The Short Story
Wrote ads at advertising agency McCann-Erickson in London. Eventually, they made him Creative Director. He also set up Magic Hat, McCann's youth agency. He was Creative Director of that too. It opened offices in ten countries.

He wrote and directed ads for Coca-Cola, Microsoft, Nescafe, MTV, VH1, Sharp and Rolling Rock. He created many campaigns for clients. Some were grateful. He kept himself busy.

Then he left, said he wanted to concentrate on directing commercials and writing some screenplays. He directed ads for clients like Honda, Sony and Government Drink Drive. He wrote and directed short films for fashion designers Frost French and Katarzyna Szczotarska. He has written some screenplays. Still busy

His most recent short film Come Here Today starring Rhys Ifans and Rita Tushingham was short listed at a number of film festivals.

Paul Wilson
The Short Story
Paul cut his teeth at AMV.BBDO in the late 90's as the advertising business was experiencing a media revolution. Worked on media planning with J Sainsbury, Volvo, Pepsi Co & BT before deciding to switch to the client side and experience brand management first hand with Bass Brewers.

The next few years were a marketing rollercoaster ride, working as part of the Hooch launch team that swiftly became one of the fastest alcohol launches in UK history.

After this, Paul joined ?What If!, the world's number one innovation company where he was a senior partner working with organisations such as Unilever, GlaxoSmithKline and Heinz. He also worked on the venture capital side of this business launching new brands from scratch in both profit and not-for-profit sectors.

Paul and Simon founded Make Believe to pursue their passion for storytelling in the commercial world. Make Believe works with clients such as the BBC, Grolsch, Carling, The Home Office, Microsoft and Novartis, helping them discover and then articulate the best possible story for their brands and organisations. They are both currently searching out the next big thing in storytelling. They are busy.

The story continues... what's yours? Join us at www.toldstory.com.

Art Director Alan Aboud
Design by Carl Wellman at ABOUD CREATIVE
Edited by Vicky Hayward and Julia Booth-Clibborn

Black and white printing by Peter Guest at The Image

First published in 2009 by Booth-Clibborn Editions
in the United Kingdom
www.booth-clibborn.com

The information in this book is based on material supplied to Booth-Clibborn Editions by the authors. While
every effort has been made to ensure accuracy, Booth-Clibborn Editions does not under any circumstances
accept responsibility for any errors or omissions.

A cataloging-in-publication record for this book is available from the publisher

ISBN 978-1-86154-304-2

Printed and bound in China

Thanks To
Alan, Mary, all at Make Believe and all our clients, everybody at Aboud Creative, Maja Flink, Robert Clarke,
Edward Booth-Clibborn, Tracy Le Marquant at Karla Otto, Jason Tasker at Metro Imaging, Joy Bryant,
Emma Comley, Lucy Yeomans, Tom Usher, SA Studio LA